Praise for Tom Daly's

The ADHD Solution for Teachers: How To Turn Any Disruptive Child Into Your Best Student

This book is a wonderful tool, and as a teacher working with emotionally disturbed, at-risk students, I found its lessons almost more valid than my actual credential education. No kidding!
—Lara Hershkowitz, San Diego, California

This book had a tremendous impact on both my sanity and a particular third-grade student. . . . We are nearing the end of the school year and I am still spending extra time with this student, not out of desperation, but because I truly enjoy his company. Thanks for the help!
—Suzanne Vaira, 3rd grade teacher, Las Vegas, Nevada

I already finished reading the book the first time. I intend to read it a second time, as recommended. I have already used some of the techniques on my son Blake. They really work!! We went over your material on "listening." It was my own fault for never teaching him how to listen. DUH!!
—Christine Curtis, LaPorte, Indiana

Thanks for your brilliant book. I can already tell that the next thirty years until retirement are going to be significantly easier and more rewarding thanks to you. How is it that your common sense wasn't common to anyone else?
—Drew Smoller, Selden, New York

What I liked best about the book was that it applies to all students, not just ADHD children. The concepts can be used across the board in any teaching situation.
—Brandi Wharton, Encinitas, California

Also by Tom Daly

Unlocking the Gifted Student Inside Your ADHD Child.

The ADHD Solution for Teachers in Action (seminar DVD)

www.adhdsolution.com

The ADHD Solution:

How To Turn Any Disruptive Child Into Your Best Student

Tom Daly

The ADHD Solution: How To Turn Any Disruptive Child Into Your Best Student

Copyright© 2005
Tom Daly

Smarty Pants Publications
8124 Paseo Del Ocaso
La Jolla, CA 92037
Tel 858-551-8416
Email adhdsolution@aol.com

www.adhdsolution.com

ISBN 0-9749870-090000

Second Edition

Printed in the United States of America

Table of Contents

A Note on the Format
of this Book

The ideas in this book were collected and developed during my 15 years of teaching children with ADD, ADHD and other learning disabilities. During that time, I had many conversations with parents and teachers that helped refine my methods. In the end, I discovered which techniques worked and which ones did not.

I wanted to share my ideas with a wider audience. So, in 2000, I teamed up with Bill Mueller, a freelance writer who shared my interest in putting these concepts into book form.

We made an interesting discovery as we explored the material together — we learned that the concepts "came alive" most effectively during our back-and-forth conversations as Bill asked questions and I explained what I had learned in teaching ADHD children over the years.

We soon discovered that the most direct way to help other teachers learn these ideas was by permitting them to "eavesdrop" on these conversations I had with Bill. That's why you'll find much of this book is presented in a question-and-answer format. It simply became the best way to convey the material.

The Q&A format not only makes the book more practical and readable, but it also resembles the seminar format in which these ideas have been presented so successfully in the past. In this way, the text seems to intuitively anticipate the reader's questions as it goes along, and provides deeper insight into each topic.

We also found that this format created a leaner, more hands-on book. We found ourselves weary of other books that forced readers to wade through reams of irrelevant information. This book avoids that problem and has effectively distilled all my best practices into one, ready-to-use manual. Enjoy!

Introduction

There is a Catch-22 in the profession of teaching so profound and pervasive that I am amazed teachers are allowed to complete the credentialing process without ever learning how to specifically solve this essential dilemma.

That dilemma is the reason I wrote this book.

And the dilemma is this:

Teachers are trained to deliver information to students who will sit still and listen — and then they're put in front of classrooms with students *who won't sit still and listen!*

Does anyone else see a problem here?

There's not a teacher alive who hasn't felt the frustration of trying to manage a classroom with at least one student who repeatedly pulls other students off-task with annoying, disorderly behavior. Whether that student is leaving his seat without permission, tapping his pencil incessantly, or putting his head down in apparent surrender, it's clear that students aren't the only victims in this dance of disruption.

You, the teacher, become a victim as well.

I've made this subject my mission not only to help students of all types, but also as a way to keep teachers refreshed and excited about their vocation. I know from experience how a single student can ruin your entire day in less than five minutes. I've also felt the joy of seeing disruptive children become my very best students.

That's right — the title of this book is not an empty promise. It's what you will literally create as you implement the deceptively simple and powerful techniques in this book.

You really *can* turn any disruptive child into your best student. This book shows you how.

This material was developed over 15 years of teaching ADHD children of all types. While you will read more about my background and how I developed these techniques in the first section of this book, let me say for now that I gained unusual insight to this problem by teaching some of the most pronounced ADHD children in my school district.

By necessity, I was forced to find a way to reach students that other teachers had given up on. At first, I made mistakes and became frustrated. But then, over time, I discovered methods for reaching kids that were simple, easy and effective. I watched some of the most un-teachable children become my best students. This book will help you achieve the same results.

There's another reason I gained unusual insight into the problem of ADHD children: I was one of those kids myself. ADHD was not a highly recognized condition back then, but you'll read how my experience as a child with ADHD shaped my life and directed my career.

When I first began looking for help on this subject, I searched everywhere for tips on how to teach children with ADHD. I found lots of information on how to recognize ADHD children, how to medicate them, how to discipline them, and how to accept them — everything except how to *teach* them.

This book does exactly that. You'll not only be helping your students, but you'll learn more about yourself in the process and grow right along with them.

It has been said that when the student is ready, the teacher will appear. It is with that same spirit of wisdom that I welcome you to "The ADHD Solution."

CHAPTER 1

How to use this book: an overview

BILL MUELLER:
How do we use this book?

TOM DALY:
Each person will apply this book differently. It is meant as a practical, hands-on guide that will demonstrate the best approach in dealing with ADHD children in all school situations. Whether it's getting him[1] to focus on his work, talking and interacting with him, setting up lesson plans or talking with his parents, this book will supply the right tools so that you'll know what approach to take with an ADHD child in any situation.

This book provides teachers with the most effective overall approaches to use, along with tricks of the trade that really work. I have been educating and guiding some of the most pronounced ADHD students day in and day out for 15 years. Through my own experiences, sharing ideas with other teachers, and continuing education, I have assembled or collected many practical techniques that are either free or cost very little that teachers can implement immediately to eliminate ADHD behaviors in their classrooms.

---

[1]Editor's Note: Please note that in many instances throughout this book we must use the pronoun of "he" or "she" in discussing hypothetical examples of ADHD children. For the sake of clear writing, and perhaps in defiance of politically correct grammar, you will find that we have, in just about every case, used the pronoun of "he" instead of using the more inclusive "he or she" or the always awkward "he/she." The fact that ADHD students are predominantly male made this an easy editorial decision.

I can almost assure you that anyone who reads this book will receive at least five "Wow-that's-a-great-idea!" discoveries.

It's critical that you have a mindset of trust when you put these techniques into practice. These strategies work. If you don't approach this material with an open-minded sense of curiosity, and a determination to make use of these strategies, then it will not work for you.

The important thing is to practice these ideas right away.

I can't stress that enough. Don't make this just an interesting book to read. This book will have tremendous value when you put it into practice. The great thing is, you can employ these techniques anywhere —not just in the classroom.

Read the entire book twice! Keep a pen and paper handy to jot down notes during both readings. And keep the book handy as a reference guide throughout the year. You'll also want to take a look at the resource section to use as a springboard to further your education.

My first year of teaching was a real struggle. I began to doubt my abilities as their teacher. I thought, "Maybe I am the problem." When I found your site, I was intrigued by the ideas presented there. Everything you were talking about was affecting me not only professionally but also emotionally. I was wondering why I became a teacher, and thinking of other career opportunities to pursue. I ordered your book and DVD and it has really helped change my perspective of my students. I was so shocked the first day of class that I went into defensive mode. I became a very angry person and I thought that I had to be really strict in order to get control. It didn't work. The kids quickly began to see my weakness. I had to start implementing some of your ideas. I am so glad that I did. By the end of the semester things were running much smoother. There was a mutual respect that was being built.

Samantha Way, Grades 9-10, Ontario, Canada

I often asked my graduate students one question: "What's the biggest room in the world?" After listening to responses such as the Taj Majal, I tell them with a smile, "The biggest room in the world is the room for self-improvement — we can all use a few great ideas!" In sharing this material with others, I always point out that "We know more than me" — in other words, my ideas only serve as a point of departure so that teachers can customize my concepts to their own particular classroom and spin them into something even more useful.

This is not a book in which I lay out a rigid system to be copied to the letter. That doesn't exist because each student is an individual and each classroom is unique. No matter your own personal teaching style, it will blend in with my proven techniques.

Most readers of this book will find themselves making a crucial shift: instead of taking an adversarial approach, they will adopt an understanding that goes something like this, "How can I redirect the energy of this child so that everyone in the classroom is learning and I can go home feeling refreshed instead of exhausted?"

BILL:
Why is this book important?

TOM:
Well, ADHD is a significant issue in every classroom today. But I also want to point out something important: many people think that ADHD is a myth, that it's simply a result of bad parenting, bad teaching, poor support, and that kids act this way on purpose.

Now whether you lean that way in your thinking or believe that ADHD is a concrete condition, the fact remains that we have large numbers of kids exhibiting these behaviors: impulsivity, blurting out verbally, hyperactivity, getting out of their seats and inattentiveness, among other things.

Here's my point: these techniques will work with these students whether you think ADHD is something of a myth or not! They get results, and that's what really matters.

13

Now, to answer your question, I think this book is valuable for three reasons.

1. Teachers are stressed out.

It only takes one or two children with ADHD in an otherwise well-run class to drain much of the teacher's time and energy. ADHD students stray off-task not only from their own work, but they pull other kids off-task, too.

Obviously, this wastes a lot of time. Here's a quick example: Years ago, before I discovered some of these techniques, I found myself saying the names of my ADHD children over and over. You know, "Joey, Joey get back to work!" Then I realized that just by saying Joey's name I might be making the problem worse. Why? People love hearing their own name. It's a form of recognition, even if the attention being garnered isn't positive. Dale Carnegie once wrote that the sweetest sound in the world is a person's own name.

For a school-aged child, you can magnify that ten-fold. Incidentally, Carnegie also said that the most common word you'll hear in a phone conversation is the word "I." We know that people are ultimately interested in themselves. Now that may not qualify as a major revelation, but I drew on that insight to realize that my repeated usage of Joey's name was actually working against me even though I thought I was punishing him!

In other words, Joey will not interpret my admonishment of "Joey, Joey get back to work!" as punishment — on some decisive level he's going to interpret that as attention.

2. Students are stressed out.

I remember a day I walked my daughter home from first grade, and I asked her how her day went. She said with a heavy sigh, "Well, it was all about Ryan again — he had his name on the blackboard with three check marks next to it." I mean, here's a first-grader who already realizes that the class is, essentially, not being run by the teacher but by Ryan. And she was feeling enough anxiety about it to mention it to me right away. You can bet that your compliant

14

students are feeling that stress, too, if your children with ADHD are not being handled properly.

3. ADHD students are stressed out.

Why is this book important? Put yourself in the shoes of a child with ADHD. ADHD kids have the same basic human and legal rights to learn and grow as all the so-called "good kids." Sometimes they try so hard, but it seems like they always fail. That's why we need to think outside the box and come up with creative solutions. Now I'm not talking about a loosey-goosey approach in which you excuse away inappropriate behavior from students with ADHD. I'm talking about providing concrete techniques to prevent problems, as well as handling consequences when problems do occur.

Here's another point to consider:

If the traditional methods worked so well, then why are we even talking right now about this subject? The fact is that too many children with ADHD are not learning what they need to, for whatever reason.

As we know, children with problems are often shuffled upward from one grade to the next, without mastering last year's content.

If that child grows older without learning what he needs, there's a higher likelihood that he will

> *The payoff for reaching children with ADHD is that our classrooms operate smoothly: the other kids learn what they're supposed to, the teachers don't burn out, and every child eventually finds his place in society.*

experience all sorts of life problems, ranging from sleep disorders to problems with law enforcement. ADHD students who learn and graduate are likely to avoid those kinds of problems. They are employable, stay out of trouble with the law, and lead independent, successful lives.

It makes sense for us to find a way to reach our kids who experience difficulties, and to make learning meaningful for them.

The payoff for reaching children with ADHD is that our classrooms operate smoothly: the other kids learn what they're supposed to, the teachers don't burn out, and every child eventually finds his place in society.

This book is not a specific method, but an effective mindset. It provides techniques based on that mindset. These are revolutionary ideas, and by revolutionary I mean to say that these techniques offer an improved way of doing things — faster, better and cheaper. These ideas are infinitely less expensive than some of the programs already operating.

Apply the concepts in this book and you won't have ADHD episodes that last a half-hour, or even five minutes. And you won't have kids getting out of their seats repeatedly during a class. Using these tips, it might happen only once per instructional period.

Instead of experiencing a problem that would ruin your day and disrupt your classroom, you can expect problems to become smaller and more manageable when you use this book.

In fact, this book will not only greatly diminish your classroom-related problems, but it will often be the ADHD student *himself* who will act as the agent of change and become your biggest helper. That's a dramatic turnaround! As the student's self-esteem rises, along with his new view of the class, his standing will also rise among his classmates. His turnaround will be a full 180 degrees.

BILL:
What other benefits can teachers expect from this book?

TOM:
Well, for starters, teachers will go home feeling better. When you're a teacher feeling stressed out after a tough day, it's often not a matter of *what's* wrong with you, but a matter of *who's* wrong with you. In other words, it's often just one or two kids who can make your day

difficult. And, invariably, those one or two kids are children with ADHD.

Teaching is a lot like being a performer: you're on stage, you're delivering a message in front of an audience, and that is taxing work. Nobody expects a stand-up comedian or a rock singer to perform for 30 to 40 hours every week, but that's our expectation for teachers.

BILL:
How many students with ADHD and ADD are we talking about? How widespread is this issue in classrooms today?

TOM:
I think the most material statistic is this: Teachers can expect at least two kids with severe ADHD symptoms in each classroom. That may include kids who blurt out, are out of their seats, and doing a variety of things that completely disrupt your classroom. You can also expect *another* two or three children who exhibit some other sort of ADHD behavior — for instance, you begin speaking a sentence and some children will finish it out loud for you because they don't have

---

☀ *Chalk Talk*

Hello, I loved your book! I teach half-time in a third grade/fourth grade combo classroom. I was getting frustrated with one particular child. I read your book about feeling frustrated and out of control and not wanting to be. I apologized to Samuel the next day for getting frustrated with him. We had a huge class discussion. Everyone was relieved. The other students just wanted to help him. At that moment, together, we came up with "monkey tokens" — two per day. When Sam is feeling like he needs to walk around, he can simply use one of these tokens to get out of his seat, go down to the office, say hello to our principal, walk down the hall, and come back. He is then required to take his seat. It has worked extremely well. The others actually remind him to take a walk with kindness! Thank you!

Tania W., Marathon, Ontario, Canada

17

the attention span to sit there and listen to your entire sentence. They are inattentive.

Some of your students with ADHD will be so stressed out because they can't process what you're saying that they simply lay their heads on their desks. Or, conversely, some will continually tap their pencil, or do other annoying things.

It's simply against their nature to process information that way — so we have to find a way that lets them somehow. These techniques will allow your ADHD kids to realize, "Hey, I *can* do this."

BILL:
Tell me about your experience in developing these techniques. I understand you've been encouraging other teachers to implement these methods for quite a while.

TOM:
I've taught these methods as a college professor to hundreds of teachers earning their masters degrees and teaching credentials. I've taught general education teachers how to deal with special education students who have been mainstreamed into their classes. So I have quite a bit of experience teaching these methods to teachers

> **Here's the problem: The one thing that school requires of students is that they sit still and listen to what the teacher is saying — and the one thing that most kids with ADHD *can't* do is sit still and listen.**

at all levels — from pre-school all the way up to adult education. I've also taught this material to those who work at day treatment facilities, residential facilities and prisons. That alone indicates how widespread this problem is.

BILL:
Why have you made this subject your mission?

TOM:
For one thing, I have experienced the havoc created by students with ADHD in a classroom setting. I've seen how they destroy your best intentions.

It amazed me that teachers can go through their credentialing and not learn about these types of strategies. A teacher's training focuses on how to deliver information to students who will sit still and listen . . . and then we're put in front of classrooms of students who *won't sit still and listen!*

And so we drive home frustrated, wondering, "Why did I ever go into teaching?" or, "Am I really cut out for this?" or, "If only those two ADHD kids weren't in my class, everything would be perfect." So I decided to create a program that would reduce teachers' stress and increase their efficacy.

BILL:
I understand you were a child with ADHD yourself.

TOM:
Yes, and that's another reason that I have made this my mission. I was a hyperactive kid who was later classified as being gifted. And I remember all the struggles I went through because I wasn't able to sit still and listen. So I understand the problem from both ends. I remember teachers getting upset at me, some of them telling me to go out and run five laps in an attempt to calm me down.

BILL:
What does it feel like to be that type of kid? It must be frustrating.

TOM:
It is! It's awful. You want to be anyplace but in the classroom. You

Chalk Talk

One of the things that really stuck in my head is that I need to not stress out my students. I love the analogy that you gave in the video about teachers getting stressed out by the principal. I never really thought of it that way until you gave that example. Now, I am more conscious of my own behavior and I know that stressing my students out will not do any good.

—Julie, Garden Grove, California

want to be out running around and doing anything except what the teacher is telling you to do. Now every student feels that tendency from time to time, *but the difference with the ADHD child is control.* Children with ADHD are not thinking, "I think I'll sit here and tap my pencil a thousand times so that I can disrupt the class." They're not thinking, "I'm going to keep blurting out in class; I'm going to keep jumping out of my seat." They're doing it without any premeditation because they have poor control. Thankfully, we can solve that.

Whether the child with ADHD is gifted or learning disabled, the common feeling ADHD kids experience is that their minds are racing 100 mph and their bodies want to *go* 100 mph. That's a recipe for trouble when you place that kid in a situation where he's supposed to be quiet and attentive.

So, a big reason I wrote this book is because I was one of those kids. ADHD wasn't an identifiable problem back then, but it was clear to me as a child that teachers didn't want me in their classes. However, I also remember that in sixth grade I tested as having college-level reading skills and that my math skills were advanced by three grades. I'm pointing that out because some kids with ADHD are in the same situation. Incidentally, in dealing with my behavior as a student, some of my teachers stumbled across a few tricks that worked, almost by accident, and I will share them in this book.

Using cross-aged tutoring is a quick example: In sixth grade I was

☀ *Chalk Talk*

Your book helped to make me less stressed out. A light bulb just went one and said, "Really, I'm not supposed to work this hard!"

—Lisa S., Milwaukee, Wisconsin

sent down to the second grade to tutor younger students with their reading. I happened to be an excellent tutor for those kids who were having a little trouble reading, and it became a win-win situation for both the second and sixth-grade teachers.

BILL:
So the good news is that there are many kids with ADHD who *can* end up leading productive, successful lives?

TOM:
Yes, absolutely, and I am living proof. I'm an ADHD kid who ended up becoming a success. And believe it or not, I'm just beginning to settle down. I graduated from college and then I bounced around in a few different jobs, which can be typical for ADHD kids. I worked as a stockbroker, I worked in sales, and then I ended up as a teacher and college professor. And, of course, I began teaching other teachers about how to effectively deal with ADHD students. I think the hyperactivity that I had back then has now translated itself into good, productive positive energy as an adult. It's sad to say, but if you're a teacher who has to choose between a kid who's blurting out, another kid who's continually getting out of his seat, another who's tapping his pencil, and a student who's got his head down on his desk — well, the teacher will prefer the kid with his head down on his desk every time! We *love* that kid with his head on his desk because we don't have to deal with him. But of course that's no solution, either, because the student with his head on his desk may not be learning. So we need to develop ways to keep problem students alert, receptive, and well behaved so that they will learn along with everyone else.

BILL:
How did you end up teaching students with ADHD? I understand it's an interesting story.

TOM:
After I got my teaching credential, I was offered a choice: take a low-paying job as a substitute teacher, or take a much better-paying position as a contract teacher in a special day school for disturbed students that had the 110 "worst" students out of the district's total of 161,000. And by "worst" I mean to say that these kids were the most violent, aggressive, problematic, severely attention-deficit students in

the district. Well, like all of us, I had a lot of bills to pay, so I took the better-paying position. I taught two-and-a-half years in that environment. Needless to say, I learned quickly. I had no choice.

After that, I moved on to teaching high school students with attention deficit and behavioral problems. I coached sports and spent time with ADHD kids in a variety of roles and subjects. I spent a total of 15 years teaching students with ADHD.

Later, I became a college professor guiding new teachers who were about to instruct special education students for the first time. I taught special education teachers how to write behavior modification plans and how to deal with kids with behavioral or emotional issues.

☀ *Chalk Talk*

I had a student who came into my classroom already labeled from the year before. He had no self-confidence or self esteem in completing and understanding school in general. After reading your book, I was able to reach this child and I believe he reached his full potential in my classroom as he went from failing to the highest student in my class. He went from being a loner to everyone wanted to be his friend. He also went from not wanting to be touched or called upon to hugging me every day, giving me positive comments about myself/himself and the classroom activities, and raising his hand and wanting to be called upon when asked for volunteers. The child used to never smile, and after implementing your strategies, he always had a smile on his face and came into the classroom ready to learn. Your book was a miracle in my classroom.

Marie L., Apalachicola, Florida

Points to remember from Chapter 1

▶ Keep an open mind and put these strategies into practice.

▶ Jot down ideas as you read this book.

▶ This book provides teachers with the most effective overall approaches to use, along with tricks of the trade that really work.

▶ Most classrooms have at least two students with ADHD.

▶ We are trained to teach students who sit still and listen, but ADHD students often do not sit still and listen.

▶ Traditional methods have not worked well for handling children with ADHD. (If they did, your student wouldn't be giving you the same problems he gave his last teacher.)

▶ An adversarial approach is doomed to fail with ADHD students. Teachers instead need to cultivate a mindset that says, "How can I redirect the energy of this child so that everyone in the classroom is learning and I can go home feeling refreshed instead of exhausted?"

▶ ADHD students who graduate are likely to avoid a variety of life problems, ranging from sleep disorders to trouble with law enforcement, and can lead successful, productive lives.

Teacher Quick Write #1

Write about a time you were stressed out.

_____

_____

_____

_____

_____

#2   A time I reached out and helped a troubled child was . . .

_____

_____

_____

_____

CHAPTER 2

Teaching children with ADHD: what works and what doesn't

BILL:
Before we launch into specific tips and techniques, tell me about the overall approach that works for teaching ADHD kids.

TOM:
For starters, a sense of humor is critical. Also, "being real" with a student will open doors for you. It allows the student to feel closer and more comfortable with you. I know that the term "paradigm shift" is an overused phrase today, but you need to undergo a shift in your thinking to effectively deal with ADHD children.

Now let's talk about what does NOT work. **What does not work is the "tough approach."** That may surprise people, but it's a fact. Movies sometimes give us a misleading impression. Movies such as "Dangerous Minds" and "The Substitute" had some of the *nicest* bad kids a real-life teacher could dream of! Hollywood has a way of sanitizing certain elements, and I will tell you from experience that I would have *loved* teaching supposedly "bad kids" like the ones depicted in those movies.

If getting tough achieved lasting results, then traditional teaching methods would have worked for these difficult kids all along, and the fact is that they simply don't.

I've read countless books on behavior modification and teaching strategies. All of the authors of those books promote consistent, organized and fair-minded class management. However, those same authors caution that the tough approach is a dangerous plan. As UCLA researchers have so elegantly stated, "There are no excess kids." And when we blindly march down the road of detention, suspension and expulsion, when we up the ante over and over without focusing on replacement behaviors and building a solid teacher-student relationship, our "get tough and hope" approach is ineffective.

So you must try other techniques with ADHD kids. **Don't think in terms of** *confronting* **or** *controlling* **their behavior. What you want to do is to anticipate and** *manage* **their behavior.** Think of molten lava flowing out of a volcano. You'd be crazy to stand in front of that flow and try to stop it, or even control it. There's no force that can stop that. But maybe you can divert that energy or redirect it so that it causes fewer problems — or even create a situation that works in your favor.

Another key is to always consider the point of view of the ADHD student. Put yourself in his shoes. I'm not suggesting a permissive approach by saying that. I advocate that mindset because it flat-out works. **Remember that each type of behavior you see from an ADHD student is a form of communication.** He's trying to communicate something to you, whether it's through the incessant tapping of his pencil, getting out of his seat, or whatever. It's your job to figure out

Remember that each type of behavior you see from an ADHD student is a form of communication. He's trying to communicate something to you. It's your job to figure out what need he is expressing to you, and one way to do that is to see life from his perspective.

what need he is expressing to you, and one way to do that is to see life from his perspective.

BILL:
How come the tough approach doesn't work with ADHD kids?

TOM:
It doesn't work because your ADHD kids are coming from a different mindset than your "Straight A" students. Those "Straight A" students see their grades and teacher approval as their "paycheck." That's why they'll work hard for a teacher's praise and good grades: because they can see and feel a payoff. But students with attention deficit or hyperactivity disorder don't see the payoff for getting good grades. They don't feel the payoff for being good. However, they know there is a payoff in acting out. The negative attention they receive is their payoff.

BILL:
Well, if the tough approach doesn't work, what does?

The typical teacher is thinking, "I need to establish control, and the students need to follow me and do what they're told." And that works just fine for most compliant students.

But it's a whole different ballgame with ADHD kids. Maybe you've heard the analogy that controlling a teenager is like mud wrestling a pig — you both get muddy and the pig enjoys it. It's much the same with trying to control ADHD kids. **You have to change your way of thinking from a controlling, adversarial mode to something more like coaching.** Think of yourself as a personal trainer for these kids.

I believe that most ADHD kids *want* to turn around. Their behavior is trying to communicate something to you, and what they're communicating to you can be boiled down to two words: "Reach me."

BILL:
I imagine the behavior of these kids can sometimes be so annoying that it would be hard to not lash back and try to control them.

27

TOM:

Yes, ADHD kids know what your hot buttons are and how to push them. But absolutely the last thing you want to enter into is a sort of verbal boxing match with these kids where you're battling back and forth, blow for blow.

Another good analogy is that of the runaway train. It's not going to work for you to stand in front of the train to stop it. Too often you put yourself squarely in front of that runaway train. But you actually contribute to the problem by trying to force some control onto a situation that is already out of control. And the unfortunate irony is, even if you do "win" that fight and gain control back through a confrontation and punishment, you go home that day feeling like you

---

☀ Chalk Talk

Sometimes it is difficult to create relationships with the children that cause you the most grief. "That one child" in my class prevented me from teaching, prevented the other children from learning, and transformed my organized, scheduled classroom into chaos. It was hard not to resent this child. The one thing that helped most with him was developing a personal, close relationship with him. I found out his interests (hunting and riding four-wheelers, if you can imagine that, for a five-year-old!). I turned my focus from controlling him to just living with his presence in my classroom! After about a month, I found that we were actually getting work done, and he would begin to focus on small tasks, simply to please me. **"Do it!" failed miserably, where "Hey, let's work on this because I really need you to help me finish this activity" succeeded. He and I had a connection. He actually cared, since I cared.** This child was not going to be considered for first grade at our private school, and thanks to this one technique I learned from your book, he is on our roll for this fall. He has also changed from a thorn in my side to a child who is very dear to my heart. I actually get defensive when other teachers "discuss" his behavior. Thank you!

Julie W., Canton,

did get run over by that train.

You can't operate like that, day in and day out, without suffering stressful after-effects. Every teacher who has battled a problematic student knows what I'm talking about.

BILL:
Then how *do* you stop this runaway train?

TOM:
Don't let the train pick up momentum in the first place. That's the first thing. You put blocks under the wheels to prevent the train from moving. However, if the train is in motion, you need to intervene quickly before it picks up too much steam. See, you have to realize that these annoying little behaviors — whether it's pencil-tapping, blurting out or whatever — means the train has already picked up speed and is heading downhill. Most teachers, when they see this happening, just want that kid out of their classroom as quickly as possible. They don't want anything to do with them.

> *If the child knows with certainty that you will react in a dramatic way if he acts out, then who's really in charge of your class?*

But that's exactly why you need to move closer to that student before he "picks up speed." That's how you place the blocks under the wheels — you anticipate problems by moving physically closer to your student.

I'm talking about establishing a closer physical proximity. No matter what your student's behavior is communicating, physical proximity can work wonders in solving it. We'll discuss specific techniques on proximity later in the book.

BILL:
Can you give us an example of using proximity?

TOM:
When I show an educational movie in class I sit between my two severe ADHD students. There is nothing threatening or imposing about it. It is very relaxed, as I just pull up a chair. But I am there,

quietly sitting between them as we watch the movie. And everyone watches that movie and follows along without incident, including those two kids. My physical presence sitting between them makes all the difference.

The key is to *act but not react*. That's part of the mental shift we have to make. If the child knows with certainty that you will react in a certain dramatic way if he acts out, then who's really in charge of the class? The student is! And do you think the other students know that? Absolutely!

Here's another way to look at it. What do you get when you place a 13-year-old ADHD child with a teacher who has seven years' teaching experience? Answer: a child that has *six more years of experience* at being ADHD than the teacher has in dealing with this sort of behavior! He's experienced, and the teacher might not be, so the student is going to play the teacher for all he can.

> **Ninety-five percent of your success in managing ADHD children has to do with what comes before a problem manifests itself.**

But if the teacher can act instead of react, that student will never stand a chance. Ninety-five percent of your success in managing ADHD children has to do with what comes *before* a problem manifests itself. If you properly set the table, your ADHD student will never feel the need to disrupt the class.

BILL:
What would you say to a teacher who's reading this but thinking that making this sort of shift is too liberal or would result in chaos?

TOM:
I would say: Do not be deceived into thinking that this approach diminishes your authority with your class. It actually gives you more.

BILL:
Why is that?

TOM:

Because all the kids know that when Johnny does something to make you react, Johnny is the one really running the class. And when you prevent those "spitting contests" between you and Johnny, the rest of the class appreciates that, whether they verbalize it that way or not. And Johnny will be on your side, too, by virtue of you meeting his needs beforehand. It can reach the point where you have established such good rapport with your ADHD student that *he* encourages *other* kids to stay on-task!

The bottom line is that controlling your class by playing the heavy-handed authority figure actually diminishes your control and your credibility.

BILL:

Can you give us a real-life success story?

> *ADHD children need someone in authority they can bond with. The key to keeping them out of trouble and making them successful adults is becoming that person. It doesn't mean that you beg for their affections. But if you make real connections with them it will make all the difference in the world.*

TOM:

Sure. I had a student named Josh at that day treatment center I mentioned earlier, the one with the 110 "worst" students out of the district's total of 161,000. Well, Josh was considered the worst out of the "elite" 110.

BILL:

"Elite" almost sounds humorous when combined with "worst" . . .

TOM:

I know . . . but when I say "worst" I am not saying these are "bad" kids, by any means. By "worst" I simply mean these kids had the most pronounced ADHD behaviors. Some of these kids had severe emotional and behavioral problems, but I'm not using the word "worst" in a judgmental sense.

31

Anyway, Josh was considered the worst kid out of this bunch. He had been at the day treatment center for years. He was violent with other students, had a history of hitting teachers, was very impulsive, and he would blurt out obscenities like someone with Tourette's. He was a nightmare for any teacher. Josh had the type of ADHD that was impulsive; you knew that whenever he hauled off and punched another kid or shouted an obscenity that he did those things without even thinking first.

BILL:
How did you manage to teach him?

TOM:
I spent some time finding out his interests. We'll talk about this later, but one of the techniques that work well is finding out what the kid loves and then utilizing that to manage his behavior. Another tactic that worked with Josh was humor. Being funny was a way "into" Josh that unlocked his potential. I also assigned him tasks that built his confidence.

BILL:
You have a knack for moving closer to these students, but what about teachers who are reading this thinking, "Hey, no way am I getting closer to this type of kid!"

TOM:
Believe me, I'm just like everyone else! At first I just wanted that kid *out* of my classroom! Make no mistake; I didn't want to get near

The biggest change has been in my attitude toward the behavior of my ADHD students. It has shifted from frustration to proactive. This shift has significantly improved my reaction to a more positive one, and this has improved the atmosphere in my classrooms.

Dianne R., Worton, Maryland

this kid. But I found that by drawing closer to my ADHD kids I significantly reduced their problematic behavior. This technique became a big part of the solution.

BILL:
So how did Josh turn out?

TOM:
Well, Josh improved and he was actually — in his own "Josh way" — helping me manage my classroom! My worst nightmare became a teaching aide of sorts! Now, he still had impulsivity, but I think it's instructive to show that after years of battling teachers he was "joining" me in my cause.

That's the sort of thing that happens when you use these techniques.

ADHD children need someone in authority they can bond with. The key to keeping them out of trouble and making them successful adults is becoming that person. It doesn't mean that you beg for their affections. But if you make real connections with them it will make all the difference in the world. This interaction, in turn, will make the ADHD kid more likeable to others. And when you help an ADHD kid become likeable, the likelihood of him getting into serious trouble is reduced.

I've also taught ADHD "poster children," including a kid that *no one* thought had a chance at success. He was on probation for attempted murder. Previous teachers warned me from trying to reach this kid because he had also been arrested for attempted rape. And then there was the girl named Caroline who wouldn't speak because she had selective mutism.

The good news is that I was able to connect with each and every one of them using these techniques. This book is the result of those success stories.

☀ Chalk Talk

BILL:
Any other thoughts before we dive into specific techniques?

TOM:
Yes. Try the following exercise: just take 10 minutes and think back to when you were the same age as the kids in your class. Really take a few minutes to think about this. Write down what it feels like to be that age. Write down what you remember. An easy way to do this is to do a short, timed writing exercise. Just 10 minutes will yield a lot. Then read over what you've written and put yourself in the shoes of your current students. Are you surprised by any insights you have gained?

For example, do you remember how much control adults had over your life back then and your efforts to wrestle that control away from them. If so, remember that, regardless of the student composition in your class, you're the one with the ultimate control of your class.

BILL:
What's another good way to create this mindset?

TOM:
Another great way is by creating balance in your own life. The better-balanced life you lead, the better example you will be for your students.

Here's another great tip: never gossip about anyone. Every time you talk badly about another staff member it *will* come back to haunt you. Teaching is like being in a lifeboat in the middle of the ocean — if you get angry with someone else in the lifeboat and shoot the flare gun at them, you're likely to sink yourself along with everyone else.

In this business, you often come across the same students, colleagues and administrators after you thought you have left them behind. Gossip will come back to haunt you every time. So don't do it. You'll feel better about yourself in the process. Instead, avoid gossip-mongers and focus 100 percent on your class and your kids!

BILL:
Any other overall mindset tips you can share?

TOM:
Yes. This may sound obvious, but it's incredibly powerful when put to use: **The only person you can control is yourself.** You can certainly do things to create a more perfect classroom, and some of those things will directly influence the behavior of your students, but remember that the only person you can control 100 percent of the time is yourself.

If you understand that, then you will carry yourself in a manner that will yield much better results.

Here's a quick example. When a kid confronted me recently, I wanted to say all sorts of confrontational things. My natural impulse was to rip into him for not following directions. Instead, I used a proven technique, "The Stoplight," which I will describe later in the book. It immediately turned a bad situation into a good one.

My point is that I was confident because I was operating from a place where I know that I am the only person I control. So, instead of employing some reactive strategy to force control, I used one of the techniques in this book. You'll find that you can handle a variety of situations by using the techniques in this book.

Teacher Quick Write #3

When I was the same age as my students
I remember . _____

_____

_____

_____

_____

#4 One way I could improve the payoff for

being on-task is by _____

_____

_____

_____

#5 I will create more balance in my own life right

now by _____

_____

_____

Points to remember from Chapter 2

▶ Don't stand in front of a runaway train!

▶ If you always confront ADHD students with the "tough approach," you'll go home tired and question your choice of profession.

▶ Changing your teaching approach from an adversarial mode to something more like coaching will not diminish your authority — it will actually enhance your authority.

▶ Always consider the point of view of the ADHD student.

▶ Know that most ADHD children want to turn around.

▶ Understand that all misbehavior is an attempt to communicate something to you, and usually that can be boiled down to two words: "Reach me."

▶ Ask yourself, "What is this child trying to communicate with this behavior?"

▶ Once you establish rapport with an ADHD student, he will encourage other students to stay on-task.

▶ ADHD children need someone in authority they can bond with. The key to keeping them out of trouble and making them successful adults is becoming that person. However, don't beg for their affections.

► Drawing closer to ADHD students will reduce their disruptive behaviors. So, use closer physical proximity to anticipate problem behaviors.

► Act; don't react.

► Take a few minutes and write down any memories you have of being the same age as your ADHD students.

► Remember that, regardless of the student composition, you are the one with the ultimate control of your class.

► Create balance in your own life.

► Understand that the only person you can control is yourself.

Teacher Quick Write #6

Think back to when you were the same age as the kids in your class. If you are not currently teaching, think about the kids you serve, or plan to serve. Really take a few minutes to think about this and write down what it feels like to be that age.

_____

_____

_____

_____

_____

_____

CHAPTER 3

What is ADHD?

BILL:
What exactly is Attention Deficit Hyperactivity Disorder?

TOM:
To start to understand ADHD, we should look at two things: We should quickly review the formal definition of ADHD, then we should talk about specific ADHD traits teachers may see in their kids.

So let's start with the following definition from the American Psychiatric Association, which has identified several characteristics that may indicate attention deficit hyperactivity disorder. These characteristics must appear before age seven, persist for at least six months, be present in more than one environment, i.e. home, school, work, etc., and there must be "clear evidence of clinically significant impairment in social, academic, or occupational functioning."

The identifying characteristics are offered in two main categories: "Inattention," and "Hyperactivity-Impulsivity."

The DSM IV definition of Attention-Deficit Hyperactivity Disorder (ADHD) is:

A. Either (1) or (2):

    (1) Inattention

Six (or more) of the following symptoms of inattention have persisted for at least six months to a degree that is maladaptive and inconsistent with developmental level:

(a) often fails to give close attention to details or makes careless mistakes in schoolwork, work, or other activities;

(b) often has difficulty sustaining attention in tasks or play activities;

(c) often does not seem to listen when spoken to directly;

(d) often does not follow through on instructions and fails to finish schoolwork, chores, or duties in the workplace (not due to oppositional behavior or failure to understand instructions);

(e) often has difficulty organizing tasks and activities;

(f) often avoids, dislikes, or is reluctant to engage in tasks that require sustained mental effort (such as schoolwork or homework);

(g) often loses things necessary for tasks or activities (e.g. toys, school assignments, pencils, books, or tools);

(h) is often easily distracted by extraneous stimuli;

(i) is often forgetful in daily activities.

(2) Hyperactivity-Impulsivity

Six (or more) of the following symptoms of hyperactivity-impulsivity have persisted for at least six months to a degree that is maladaptive and inconsistent with developmental level:

Hyperactivity

(a) often fidgets with hands and feet or squirms in seat;

(b) often leaves seat in classroom or in other situations in which remaining seated is expected;

(c) often runs about or climbs excessively in situations in which it is inappropriate (in adolescents or adults, may be limited to subjective feelings of restlessness);

(d) often has difficulty playing or engaging in leisure activities quietly;

(e) is often "on the go" or often acts as if "driven by a motor";

(f) often talks excessively;

Impulsivity

(g) often blurts out answers before questions have been completed;

(h) often has difficulty awaiting turn;

(i) often interrupts or intrudes on others (e.g. butts into conversations or games).

Is ADHD a myth?

Some people think ADHD doesn't exist, while others consider it a real, identifiable medical condition. You'll see educators and physicians across the spectrum on this issue. Some say that ADHD is just poor parenting, or bad teaching. Others claim it's just kids with a lot of energy, which is normal since many kids just can't sit still for six hours a day.

To add to the debate, the National Mental Health Institute has concluded that visual differences in the brain activity of ADHD students can be found through MRI data. After spending hundreds of hours of research, I believe that ADHD is a real, identifiable medical condition. However, every educator must come to his or her own conclusion.

What I do know is that we have children in our classrooms who fidget, blurt out, and cannot pay attention. Most important to me is that educators try strategies to reach these children. Whether teachers feel ADHD is "real" or not is not my immediate concern.

An ADHD child may experience problems with attention, be distractible, or act hyperactive. One determining factor is that *the behavior is not age-appropriate.*

How to recognize ADHD in your students

BILL:
Let's say I'm a brand new teacher. How would I recognize a child with ADHD?

TOM:
You're looking for a few different things. Now understand that not all ADHD kids will have all of these traits. This is just a list of possible characteristics.

Some of the following traits will apply to the kids you teach, and some may not:

- **"Un-likeability."** Sometimes kids with ADHD make it hard for you to like them. Staff and administrators do not like them, and they're sometimes un-likeable to their peers.

- **A child who is "attention-needy."** This child constantly needs your attention. Typically the child with ADHD will grab your attention in a negative way. Why? Because if an ADHD kid quietly works, he might receive your attention. But if he throws something in the classroom he is *guaranteed* to get your attention! So it is more efficient for him to act out. When we talk about attention-needy kids, I bring up the following example. Do you remember as a kid when you'd be eating so much and someone would say, "Where does he put it all? He must have a hollow leg." Well, I've heard it said that the ADHD kid has a hollow heart. And no matter how much love or attention you give him, he needs more and more.

42

- **The inability to handle unstructured free time.** A lot of ADHD kids "don't do nothing well." That means it's not a good idea to give those children nothing to do. For instance, rewarding ADHD students with "free time" as a way to fill your school day is not a good idea. Let's say you had a great lesson and there's only four minutes to go before the bell, and you decide the four minutes would be a perfect opportunity for you to quickly check your school email. It's fine to give the class the four minutes of free time as a group reward, but you better assign your ADHD students a specific task, whether it's puzzles, searching on the Internet, or whatever. The free time needs to have a directed activity involved in some way, or you're asking for trouble from your ADHD kids.

- **A child who appears to have "gaps" in his learning.** This child, for example, may score low on tests, but you notice that during class you're able to hook his interest, he knows many of the answers and you can tell he gets the material. What often happens in this case is that the child has gotten older each year but because he can't pay attention very well, he's not learning the actual content that the other kids are learning. So, in this situation, you might have a kid who's brilliant, but his achievement is far below what you would expect.

- **A child who crowds others.** This is where the child doesn't have an age-appropriate concept of personal space. He might get very close to you, and you find yourself telling him to back away. If you know a kid who has inappropriate space boundaries, then that might be an ADHD characteristic.

- **An "On/Off" switch in the brain.** This means they get part of it, they don't get part of it, they get part of it, they don't get part of it. It's kind of like they "get" things only intermittently.

- **A child who will rearrange procedural steps overnight on something you've taught him.** For example, maybe you taught him a mathematical equation in which he's learned that first you add A, then you add B, and then you get C. And then the next day he gets all three steps backwards. So every day you have to

43

re-teach him the same three steps. He has to re-learn school procedures and has to re-learn basic rules of math or English.

- **The "faulty connection" effect.** In these children, it seems like there is a faulty connection in the brain. You might be tempted to think that if only you could persuade a neurosurgeon to open up this child's brain, the doctor could reattach those wires and he would become okay.

- **Significant maladaptive behaviors.** A small number of ADHD students will display severe emotional or behavioral problems. This includes lying, stealing, setting fires, and an inability to accept responsibility for their actions.

Once again, understand that not all ADHD kids will have all of these traits. This is just a list of possible traits.

BILL:
How do you tell if a child truly has ADHD, or if he just enjoys acting like a brat?

TOM:
The main difference is the ability of control. If a student has control over his behaviors and he plots a way to hurt someone, then we might classify that student as having a conduct disorder. For example, let's say a kid is thinking about a way to hurt you, then plans out how to hurt you, follows through on that plan, and executes that plan without getting caught. That's more typical of a conduct disorder, and if it's serious enough, that type of behavior will eventually incarcerate a kid.

Some less severe forms of conduct problems include students who constantly are defiant and consistently test limits. Like the raptors in "Jurassic Park," it seems they will continue to systematically "test the fences" until they find a weak link and get their way.

On the contrary, a kid with ADHD doesn't have that sort of control. He may indeed do something bad, but it's almost as if he did it on impulse, without thinking first.

Points to remember from Chapter 3

▶ The American Psychiatric Association has developed a detailed definition of ADHD (refer to the list in this chapter).

▶ There is debate as to whether ADHD is a real, identifiable medical condition.

▶ Nine possible school traits of ADHD children may include students who:

- Are hard to like.
- Need unlimited amounts of attention.
- Cannot handle unstructured free time.
- Have big gaps in their achievement.
- Have no concept of age-appropriate personal space.
- Exhibit serious or dangerous behaviors.
- Only learn things intermittently.
- Need to relearn school procedures over and over.
- Seem to have a "faulty connection."

▶ The main difference between "normal" students and children with ADHD is the ability of control.

CHAPTER 4

The 90/10 Rule

BILL:
What's "The 90/10 Rule"?

TOM:
"The 90/10 Rule" says that 90 percent of your class management problems will come from 10 percent of your students. And of that 10 percent, at least a couple of those students will be ADHD kids. That means that, as a general rule, out of a class of 30 kids, about three of them are going to cause 90 percent of your problems, and at least two of the three "troublemakers" will probably have ADHD.

BILL:
Out of a classroom of 30 students, you can expect about two ADHD kids?

TOM:
Actually, in some classes, you can expect four ADHD students. And, typically, two of them will have a particularly acting-out form of ADHD. The others will likely have some sort of distractibility but it may not disrupt your classroom. These are some general numbers based on my experience.

Most experts say that between 4 and 8 percent of the school-aged population has some type of severe ADHD condition or emotional difficulties. Of that 4 to 8 percent — and it may be higher than that

— less than 1 percent are receiving any sort of special-ed services for their problems.

So my question is: Who are you more worried about, the 1 percent getting help from special-ed services, or the other 3 to 7 percent who are floating around without any help? There are at least two students in each general-ed class who need extra support. The strategies in this book are designed specifically for those students. However, these are excellent strategies for all the other students, too.

The 90/10 Rule tells you that 90 percent of your problems will come from 10 percent of your students. You *must* find a way to handle that 10 percent, and not let it handle you, or you'll never be a fully satisfied, happy and effective teacher.

If you approach it from an authoritative point of view, where your stance is "I'm bigger than you, I'm the teacher and you must listen to me," you're not going to win. You may win small battles here and there, but taking that sort of approach will take a toll on you emotionally, physically, and spiritually. It's not worth it! You can't afford to take on that type of battle. The toll is so significant, that you will go home feeling wiped out, and you'll start to hate your job. You'll never reach retirement going down that road.

> *The 90/10 Rule tells you that 90 percent of your problems will come from 10 percent of your students. You must find a way to handle that 10 percent, and not let it handle you, or you'll never be a fully satisfied, happy and effective teacher.*

If you think that handling that 10 percent in the traditional, "I'm-The-Teacher" way worked, don't you think it would have worked with the teacher before you — and the teacher before that, and the one before that?

If that approach worked, you wouldn't still be observing the same problems from these kids. All the teachers before you would have solved the problem. But they clearly have not. But, now, with this book, *you* have the chance to stop the cycle.

As teachers, we sometimes let our egos get in the way and we think, "Oh, well, I'm a much better teacher than so-and-so; I can turn this kid around, just watch me." But I'm here to tell you that the traditional way is neither effective nor efficient in turning around that 10 percent.

BILL:
So how DO you handle that 10 percent?

TOM:
You handle those students with a number of creative, non-combative ways — all of which are explained in this book. Chief among them are the following three: "Right Words" (Chapter 6), the Walk and Talk strategy (Chapter 7), and Interest Inventories (Chapter 8).

Teacher Quick Write #7

Recall a time when "that 10 percent" handled you instead of the other way around.

_____

_____

_____

_____

_____

_____

Points to remember from Chapter 4

▶ Ninety percent of your problems come from 10 percent of your students.

▶ You must find a way to handle that 10 percent, and not let it handle you, or you will never be a fully satisfied, happy and effective teacher.

▶ The traditional method of, "I'm the teacher; do what I say," will not work with many ADHD children.

▶ Use "Right Words" (Chapter 6), Walk and Talk (Chapter 7) and Interest Inventories (Chapter 8) to eliminate ADHD behaviors in your classroom.

CHAPTER 5

How to sound like a more professional teacher (and why it's so important)

TOM:

I want to talk about how to sound like a professional teacher when you're dealing with students with behavior problems. More specifically, how to *be* a professional teacher in the words you select.

BILL:

Is that really important?

TOM:

That is *so* important. Let's say you're working with students who have difficulties, such as attention deficit disorder. If you run up to the principal, or the school psychologist, or the special-ed specialist, and say, "This student's out of control; I can't handle him!", the first thing those people may think is: "Well, maybe you're a bad teacher. Maybe you don't know how to control kids." Now, the reason they're thinking this is because the words you have chosen are not helpful: *This student's out of control. This student is bad. I can't handle this kid.* Using language like that does not dissect the problem because it's too vague. It sounds like you haven't pinpointed the problem — and, if you're using language like this, means you probably haven't.

BILL:
So, specific language is needed so that your complaint will have credibility?

TOM:
Right.

BILL:
How can that be done exactly?

TOM:
Students only display four types of behavior. Becoming familiar with this hierarchy of behavior is critical in both diagnosing a problem and then discussing it with others. Parents and educators will take you more seriously, and once you are able to differentiate between which types of behavior your students are exhibiting, then you'll be able to choose a strategy to correct the situation.

Let me list the hierarchy of behaviors in order of desirability:

    1. The first level of the behavior hierarchy is called "On-Task." A student who is "on-task" is doing what you're asking him to do. When you give him directions, he's following them quickly and quietly, stays on-task and is not bothering others.

    2. The second level is called "Off-Task." While the rest of your class might be on-task doing an assignment, the student who is off-task is mostly not engaged in the task — he is off-task.

    3. The third level is called "Disruptive." The disruptive student is both off-task and is successfully pulling other students off-task. Sometimes the student is being disruptive because the work is over his head, or because a particular task seems boring.

    4. The highest level in this behavior hierarchy is "Aggressive." An aggressive student is one who is volatile and agitated, one who may get violent. Aggression can be foreseen in clenched fists, tightened jaw, and a focused expression upon a target.

Or, the student may already be acting out physically by pushing or hitting others, or by throwing objects.

BILL:
How can a teacher use these classifications to her benefit?

TOM:
Well, one important benefit is that whenever an educator discusses a student who's acting out, you will be able to immediately determine which category the student's behavior falls into, and that alone will give you a better handle on the situation. For instance, if another teacher is telling you that a student goofs off during assignments but isn't necessarily distracting other students in the process, you could

categorize that behavior as "off-task." If that's the case, there are several things you can do to correct that problem, including planned ignoring with positive reinforcement for being good. (Planned ignoring, which is discussed in Chapter 15, is withholding staff attention while a student is choosing to be off-task).

Or maybe you're being told that a student is exhibiting behaviors that sound disruptive. In that case, you'll know exactly what to do about that situation.

Using these four classifications in your verbal descriptions will make you sound credible and professional.

Teacher Quick Write #8

Give an example of a student who is:

- on task _____ __

  _____

  _____

- off task _____

  _____

  _____

- disruptive _____

  _____

  _____

- aggressive _____

  _____

  _____

Points to remember from Chapter 5

▶ Using specific language to pinpoint your student's type of behavior will give you more credibility.

▶ There are four kinds of student behavior: on-task, off-task, disruptive and aggressive.

▶ Once you understand and categorize the student's behavior into one of the four types discussed in this chapter, you will be able to choose the best strategy to correct the situation.

CHAPTER 6

The magic of 'Right Words'

BILL:
What is "Right Words?"

TOM:
Consider a boxing match. In a boxing match, the two combatants face each other, trade blow for blow, and whoever is strongest at the end wins. However, they have inflicted a lot of damage on each other in the process. Now compare this to the martial arts, in which you are taught to deflect blows and deflect that attacking energy away from you without getting hurt. That's why some karate combatants do not appear hurt even after long, drawn-out battles. They're deflecting and redirecting the other person's energy.

"Right Words" works along the same principle, except that it involves verbal situations and not physical fighting. For example, if a student is disruptive in the classroom, it is better for me to deflect his energy or redirect it rather than confront him.

If I confront students every day, I'm going home drained and discouraged.

Kids have unlimited energy, and we don't have as much in comparison. If you're always butting heads with a kid in class, how can you throw your best energy into teaching a great lesson?

BILL:
Is "Right Words" used *during* a confrontation, or to *avoid* a confrontation?

TOM:
"Right Words" is used in all sorts of situations, not just confrontational ones. When it comes to confrontations, however, "Right Words" is mostly used *before* a conflict has a chance to develop. That's where it has its greatest power. It is effective inside and outside the classroom.

BILL:
I understand the power of "Right Words" comes from the choice of language, is that right?

TOM:
Yes. The first "Right Words" technique I'd like to illustrate is this: **Eliminate the word "frustrating."** How many times does something happen to you in which your immediate mental response is, *"Isn't this frustrating!"* Using that word takes a cumulative toll on your mindset. "Frustrating" is a powerfully charged negative word that doesn't solve the problem at hand.

Using the word "frustrating" will generally make things worse.

BILL:
So what's the solution?

If you confront students every day, you're going to go home drained and discouraged.

When a student is disruptive in the classroom, it is better to deflect his energy or redirect it rather than confront him. 'Right Words' shows you how to do that.

TOM:
Simply replace the word "frustrating" with the words "fascinating" or "interesting."

That may sound ridiculously simple, but you will find that if you do this on a regular basis, the change that occurs within you is profound. It will give you an instant paradigm shift on your problem.

☼ Chalk Talk

I had a very stressful year and day-by-day became increasingly frustrated. I found the Right Words very helpful. I replaced the word "frustrating" with either "fascinating" or "interesting," which I must say described most of my situations in the classroom to a "T." One day, one of my colleagues heard me refer to a student's behavior as "fascinating." Knowing my stress level at that point, she thought I had totally lost my mind. I shared your concept with her and then she understood. I must say that changing my use of this word helped me get through the rest of my year. In fact, it became quite humorous at times, which helped me with my stress level. Thanks for an interesting way to deal with "frustrating" students and situations at school and at home.

Cathy M., Church Hill, Tennessee

BILL:
Can you give me an example?

TOM:
Let's say you're a teacher running late to work. Something has happened at home that delays you, and now you're hoping for no traffic, but then you hit a detour, and you know your class is sitting there waiting for you. And you've forgotten your cell phone, which means you can't call the school to let them know you're running late.

So now you're thinking, "Here I am two blocks from the school, and I'm hardly moving an inch. My class is sitting there all lined up and the administrators are wondering where I am. Then you say out loud, *"Isn't this . . . interesting."* Or: *"Isn't this . . . fascinating."*

Doing this seems silly, but it will reduce your stress. Using those words will help you realize the futility of worrying about a situation beyond your control.

Keep in mind it will feel uncomfortable at first. But if you stick with it, it will become second nature and you'll discover an amazing shift inside. You'll think, "Isn't this interesting? I know that my kids are lined up right now waiting for me, and I'm sitting here in traffic. And the principal has probably opened my door and is now sitting there waiting for me. This is just one of those interesting situations in life. It happens to everyone, and today is my turn."

BILL:
So "Right Words" shows us how precise words can improve our outlook?

TOM:
Absolutely. I'll give you a quick example of how effective and long-lasting this technique is: Recently, while I was visiting a new high school, I ran across a former college student. He was one of the hundreds of teachers I have taught these various techniques to. I said, "How are you doing, Robert?" And would you believe it, after not seeing him for about three years, his reply to me was, "Hey, Professor Daly, it's been . . . *fascinating.*"

BILL:
(Laughter.)

TOM:
It was priceless. And not only that, he pulled open his desk drawer to show me materials from my teachings that he was still using *daily* three years later! They're sitting in his drawer and he said he uses them all the time. They're powerful tools.

Now, that last example dealt with internal dialogue. Now let's look at an example where you're sitting in a meeting. And let's say your immediate supervisor has no experience teaching your subject, or maybe he's new to his position. And during this meeting your supervisor suggests that you try something in your class that you know absolutely will not work with your kids.

60

Your natural reaction might be to stiffen with defensiveness and frustration. *Or*, you could sit there and think to yourself, *Hmm, now isn't this interesting that this new administrator is suggesting something that I'm pretty sure won't work. Interesting. Well, let's see where it leads.*

BILL:
What I like about this approach is it allows you to be less judgmental.

TOM:
Right. When you judge something, you are narrowing your options. And when you narrow your options, your creativity goes out the window. What you need in this meeting is a little creativity. You need a creative way to redirect the energy of this well-meaning, but perhaps misguided, supervisor and convert it into a positive result.

BILL:
So, you just sit there at the meeting and passively let the bad ideas roll on?

> **When you judge something, you are narrowing your options. And when you narrow your options, your creativity goes out the window.**

TOM:
No, at some point you calmly interject "Right Words" idea No. 2 and say, "Perhaps we should consider . . ." and then you delineate your ideas. They're more likely to accept your ideas when you preface them by saying, "Perhaps we should consider . . ."

BILL:
Let's talk about how this might work in a classroom situation. Let's say you have a child with ADHD who's frustrated with an in-class assignment and he's starting to cause a problem.

TOM:
Well, when you use "Right Words" phrases you will positively affect your students. They will feed off your example.

For example, in the situation where you came to work a little late, you're inevitably going to hear teasing from some of your students

— "You're late, you're late" — but you can turn this from a negative situation into a positive one pretty easily. You can say, "You know, this was an interesting morning, and I'll tell you why . . ." You calmly discuss what happened and what choices you made that led you to being late. You could tell them what you'll have to do tomorrow to prevent it from happening again, whether it's leaving your house 15 minutes earlier, driving a different route or whatever. Your students will learn from your example by how you're handling the situation mentally and how you take responsibility in talking about it.

Use this "life example" as a teachable moment. Do this by "thinking out loud" with your class. This sets an excellent example for them in managing their own personal stress.

It's a way of putting a positive spin on a situation. We once had a parent ask our administrators to provide valet parking because parking was such a problem at our school.

BILL:
You're kidding me!

TOM:
No, this really happened! And the administrator started the dialogue by saying, "That's an interesting idea . . ." It provided an ideal bridge for deflecting an absurd idea.

BILL:
What are some other examples of "Right Words?"

TOM:
There's one I like to use a lot that I have already mentioned briefly. Let's say you're in a meeting that's going nowhere. Here's a phrase that is incredibly powerful: *"Perhaps we could consider . . ."* By the way, this is a phrase recommended in Dale Carnegie's book, "How To Win Friends And Influence People."

It's a great way to present an idea under the radar, so to speak. For example, say you're in a meeting with administrators and other team members who are doling out advice on how to handle a certain student. And let's say they're presenting ineffective ideas you know will not work. Because, after all, you've been working with this student personally and you have a much better idea as to what he will respond to. The one thing you *do* know is that what they are suggesting won't work. In fact, you know two or three things that *do* work with this student.

So, after listening to everyone's input, introduce your ideas to the group and your supervisors by saying, "Perhaps we could consider . . ." and then attach your idea to that phrase. It's a great way to turn that meeting around.

I say it this way: "After listening to everyone's ideas . . . (pause) . . . perhaps we could consider . . ."

BILL:
It seems like you put your idea across while giving them the notion that everyone came up with it as a group. Or at least that it was a collaborative process — but either way it will give your idea a better chance of success.

TOM:
Yes, exactly. And that dynamic works well with kids, too.

BILL:
What is another good use of "Right Words?"

☼ *Chalk Talk*

Your book has helped me get past some of the crazy questions students ask in the middle of class that have nothing to do with the subject. I give a short response and keep going with class. This has dramatically increased the pace of classes.

Kellie, Fayetville, North Carolina

TOM:

Sometimes kids will ask you bizarre questions. They'll ask about your personal life, or something else totally inappropriate. Some kids love embarrassing their teacher, and this is one of their favorite methods: Ask the teacher a personal question. Of course, you'll hear this from adults, too, but I'm mainly talking about students.

BILL:

What sort of questions? Will students ask you about your personal life?

TOM:

Well, it depends on the school and the age of your students. Sometimes, if you're making the kids work hard, they'll assume you're having personal problems at home and will ask you questions about that. If you show up to class tired they will think you were drinking or doing drugs, and will try to shock you with a question about that. Female teachers can be asked about their menstrual cycles. In my own case, my eyes used to get red from wearing contacts. You can imagine the students' questions about that.

Here are four things to say to a student (or an adult) that will instantly defuse the situation:

1. Simply say, "Why would you ask that?"

And then you literally walk away. Don't stand there and accept more questions. If you're in a classroom, you can say, "Why would you ask that?" and immediately move away from the student, change your body language, or direct the class to another topic. The idea is to say the sentence, then physically move on. It also works perfectly when a colleague — or any other adult — asks you an inappropriate question.

2. Say, "You know, you and I can talk about that later."

This is good for questions that may not be completely inappropriate. Follow this up by saying the student can stop by class after school to discuss it. This is also a great response to buy some time when a student puts you "on the spot."

3. Spin it around by saying, "I'm glad you asked that—" then you use their question as a point of departure to explain something you want to talk about.

This is one that I absolutely love. The phrase, "I'm glad you asked that" is the perfect bridge to make a point, correct a student's behavior, or explain something you really want to say to anyone, including adults or colleagues. The beauty of this one is that there's no protest on the other person's part because you're actually expressing gratitude for their question, *and* it also provides a platform for serving a lesson or correcting a behavior. It deflates a negative person. It's beautiful. Try it some time!

4. Directly say in a matter-of-fact tone, "That's not an appropriate question," and quickly move on to the subject at hand.

Now, let's switch gears and discuss using "Right Words" with confrontational parents. Let's say a parent confronts you and gets in your face about something. This sometimes happens. It's estimated that 5 percent of the population has some degree of emotional difficulties, which means there is a good likelihood that one or more of your students' parents are capable of such a confrontation.

The first thing to do is get up if you're sitting down, and begin walking out of the room while delivering your response.

You walk out of the meeting or classroom where this confrontation is escalating. Don't make yourself a captive audience to anyone's verbal abuse.

BILL:
That makes sense. What do you say as you're moving away?

TOM:
You say, "It doesn't look like we're going to solve this here. Let's go see Miss Farnsworth (the vice principal, or whomever it is that you need to take this to). That's where these things get solved." Remember to immediately start walking to Miss Farnsworth's office.

BILL:
What if the person doesn't follow you?

TOM:
It doesn't matter if the person follows you or not. The person is yelling at you, right? But here's the important thing: you don't want this person accusing you later of just leaving the meeting. You don't want them telling the principal later, "The teacher just walked away from me." That's why you want to have an explicit reason for what you're doing. You want to have a purpose for your destination. And you do — you're taking this situation to the proper authority figure.

BILL:
I suppose this is a smart strategy also because you don't want to just sit there and defend yourself.

TOM:
Right. You don't want to sit there and say, "Hey, I just taught for seven hours today, and your kid was the worst kid out of the whole bunch, and here you are yelling at me as if I am the one to blame!" No, instead it's much smarter and effective to say, "It doesn't look like we're going to solve this here. Let's go see Miss Farnsworth. That's where these things get solved." Then get up and move out!

BILL:
What happens when you reach Miss Farnsworth's office?

TOM:
Well, there's one more important thing to remember. Once you get there, you'll want to make an appointment with Miss Farnsworth's

assistant *for the next day*, not for right then. You can set up an arrangement with the assistant, in which he immediately knows never to schedule a same-day appointment if you use the words, "We are at an impasse."

BILL:
You don't want to meet with Miss Farnsworth right then and there?

TOM:
No. The parent in this situation is over-reacting. It's not a good time for a reasonable discussion. If you set it up for the next day, the meeting will be shorter, and you will have avoided the anger the parent is displaying at the moment. And, remember, that usually the parent who is exploding at you is not really angry with you. He or she is mad at something else. They're just taking it out on you.

So you say, "It doesn't look like we're going to solve this here. Let's reschedule this meeting with Miss Farnsworth. I'll go see when she's available." Then you see Miss Farnsworth's assistant and have her ask the parent, "Miss Farnsworth has time at 9 a.m. or 4 p.m. — which one works better for you?"

BILL:
Give us another example of "Right Words".

TOM:
Sure, here's a great one. This is something that everyone has experienced as a consumer. It's called, **"Feel, Felt and Found."** It's a technique used by sales professionals, and it's something teachers can use, too.

This is an effective way to increase the on-task time of ADHD students. Let's face it, part of teaching is convincing students to do any number of things: Do their work, do a better job and behave better. In a way, you have to "sell" students on doing their work. You're emphasizing learning over teaching.

I always focus on, "What are my students learning?" as opposed to, "How well am I teaching?" And the "Feel, Felt and Found" technique is a terrific way to accomplish this.

Now, if the sales professional is good at his job, then all three elements of the "Feel, Felt and Found" technique are spaced out so that you don't even notice what is happening. Here's the overall model:

- *I know how you feel,*
- *I've felt that way before, and*
- *Here's what I've found.*

BILL:
Okay, show me a specific example of how this works.

TOM:
Let's start with something most of us have been through: Buying a new car. You're talking to the salesman, and you say, "Look, I'd like to buy this car, but I'm worried about the payments." And the salesman who is familiar with the "Feel, Felt and Found" technique responds by saying, "Sure, I know how you feel. A car payment is a big responsibility. I felt that way myself when I bought a car here last month. It was costing me $320 per month . . . but I had an older car just like yours, and what I found was that I was spending a fair amount just on maintenance because of the repairs it needed. And it was also stressing me out, and sometimes the repair caused me to be late to work. That's when I decided a new car would be a better solution for me. I was already spending close to $300 on maintenance, and now I can drive with peace of mind because I don't have to worry about my car."

Now here's the key thing — to use this technique effectively you must spread out the three elements. You can't just rip through the "Feel, Felt and Found" parts of this in just a sentence or two. It has to evolve naturally and over a longer period of time. Otherwise the person you're talking to will feel like they're being sold something. You'll sound more genuine spreading them out.

Here's an example of how this might work in the classroom. I once taught a child named Eddie who had severe attention deficit, plus anger issues and impulsivity. It took 18 months to get through to him. After two years, I noticed he was reverting back into his old ways. He was throwing and banging things, raising his voice, and intimidating kids. In addition, he was shutting down during class.

One day, when Eddie was really irritating me, I wanted to just let him have it by saying, "Eddie, what are you doing? You're destroying my class; you're driving me crazy. I should call your parents right now and have them come get you. I've done all these great things for you," yadda, yadda, yadda. But instead, I remained silent and took him for a walk.

After a while, we started talking. I found out that two weeks earlier his uncle had died. He was very close to this uncle. They worked on cars together. The uncle lived just a few houses away from Eddie and they saw each other every day. His uncle was the one person that Eddie really connected with. During our conversation, it occurred to me that I hadn't seen Eddie eat the previous couple weeks. We had some in-class events with food, and I remembered that Eddie had never wanted anything to eat. I asked Eddie how much weight he had lost, and he said he had lost 15 pounds. He was a big kid, but that was still a lot of weight for him to lose over two weeks.

So I used "Feel, Felt and Found" with him to convince him to see a counselor that day. His parents picked him up that afternoon and took him to the counselor. He ended up graduating, and I think my conversation with him not only turned him around, but also could have saved his life.

BILL:
What did you say to him, exactly?

TOM:
After listening to him, I said, "You know, Eddie, I sort of know what you're going through because my mother died." (*I know how you feel*). Then I talked about how I felt for a while, how I felt alone and the other feelings I went through at the time (*I've felt that way before*). And then after a while, I said, "You know, I went and talked to someone about it and it really helped" (*here's what I've found.*)

By spacing those three elements out far enough, he was receptive. Toward the end of our walk I asked him, "Eddie, if your parents came here and picked you up, would you be willing to see a counselor today?" He said okay.

I want to reiterate that if you say the three elements "Feel, Felt and Found" too closely together, it will sound cheap and it won't work. I mean, can you imagine how insincere it would sound if I told him rather quickly, "Gee, Eddie, I know how you feel — my mother died and I felt pretty bad and I found that I needed to talk to someone. Would you be willing to do that?"

BILL:
It sounds as if the walk you had with him was instrumental in drawing out this information, but you're saying that this Feel, Felt Found technique also can be used right in the classroom?

TOM:
Absolutely. Here's a situation in which you can use "Feel, Felt and Found" with your entire class. Let's say you had planned a "movie day" for your students on Friday. Then you discover that the principal will be observing your classroom on that day, and she requests to see a traditional lesson at that time. So now you must inform your class that the movie has to be canceled. The kids are going to be upset, but you can use Feel, Felt and Found by saying, "Look, guys, I know how you feel . . . " Then you can tell them a story about when you were disappointed, and you can get around to saying . . . "but what I've found is that when I am being observed during a class and the students do a great job, I'm willing to ask the principal for permission to give my class something even better than we had planned as a reward, so let's talk about what we might be able to do. Who wants pizza and a movie on Monday? Okay, then let's talk about what we need to accomplish to make that happen."

BILL:
I can see how that would work. But, again, you want to space out those three elements as best you can, right?

TOM:
Yes. It's not hard to do. It's just a matter of being relaxed and being sincere.

You must practice these ideas in order for them to work. Pick one per day and see how you can put it to work. You will be amazed how well they work with a little practice. For instance, on a particular day, look to use the "Perhaps we could consider" technique. Just having it in your mind will allow you to find opportunities to use it.

BILL:
That's a good idea. Can you show us another example of "Right Words?"

TOM:
Sure. Let's say a student has asked you to drive him home and you want to deflect it. Here's something you can say in that situation which will soften any possible conflict. What you say is this (I've put the key part of this technique in italics): "*I would love to* give you a ride home because I know you're stuck. *I'm only hesitant because* it's against school rules/I have to go pick up my daughter. *Instead of that, let's call your mom from my cell phone.* See how that takes all the rejection out of it, while giving them a legitimate reason for your answer?

This technique works quickly and effectively. To recap, here are the three elements:

- *I would love to . . .*

- *I'm only hesitant because . . .*

- *Instead of that, let's . . .*

It heads off problems wonderfully. Another example might be, "Look, Ryan, **I'd love to** let you go out on a hall pass right now. **I'm only hesitant because** the principal said that during the first five minutes of the class no one is allowed to go out on a hall pass, and if they do the teacher will get into trouble. **Instead of that**, let's wait four more minutes. Do some of your work first, and then I'll let you go."

BILL:
Let's go on to another example of "Right Words".

71

TOM:

Sure. Let's say you have an ADHD student who has his head down while everyone else is working on a math assignment. What you can do is this: You walk up next to him while everyone else is quietly doing their work, and whisper to him (or quietly state) in a matter-of-fact, unemotional tone, "Jimmy, you can continue to lay there with your head down, but if you do I'll have to keep you after school today for five minutes and call your mother. Or you can start working on the math assignment right now and still earn full credit. **It's your choice.**" And then you walk away.

BILL:

I like how you end your statement to him by simply saying, *"It's your choice."*

TOM:

Right. **And then you walk away. You say everything calmly.** There's no argument here. You're simply giving him a clear choice. The great thing is, even if you walk away and hear him let out a big, complaining sigh, but then he gets to work, you basically won that situation.

BILL:

What do you do if he doesn't get back to work?

TOM:

If he doesn't get back to work, then a couple minutes later you can walk by his desk again and say, "Jimmy, it looks like you've chosen to stay after school for five minutes and for me to call your mother. I'm going to call her right now. Is she at work or at home?" Then, I call the parent right there in the classroom and say, "Mrs. Wright, Jimmy is refusing to do his math, can you talk to him for a minute?" Then I hand Jimmy the phone and say, "Jimmy, your mom wants to talk to you."

> **You must practice these ideas in order for them to work. Pick one per day and see how you can put it to work. You will be amazed how well they work with a little practice. For instance, on a particular day, look to use the "Perhaps we could consider" technique. Just having it in your mind will allow you to find opportunities to use it.**

BILL:

Either way, he's learning that he's responsible for his own actions, as well as the consequences. It also teaches the rest of the class that you are serious about their education. I'll bet the key to this one is actually following up on what you say you'll do.

TOM:

Exactly. You have to make the consequence something that you'll definitely do. For example, if you make the threat to call his mother "right away", you must follow through on that every time.

The punishment doesn't have to be exactly what I said above. Adapt this to your own classroom. Here's another example. Let's say Tim is tapping his pencil and won't stop. You can walk up to him quietly and calmly state: "Tim, you can continue to tap your pencil on the

☀ Chalk Talk

I purchased your book at the end of a very difficult school day. It gave me hope. I immediately started to use one very specific technique with my students. If a student was off-task I would simply walk over and quietly offer them choices with consequences. Then I would say, "It's your choice," and walk away. Inevitably, they would get back on-task. I was amazed at how effective this simple strategy could be, and I started to enjoy my classes more.

Kathy C., Damascus, Maryland

After reading your book I used the "It's your choice" with a student who was being disruptive in my classroom. Immediately she stopped being disruptive. She didn't begin participating, but she did stop disrupting my class immediately!

Martha C., Fredericksburg, Virginia

desk and stay after school for 20 minutes. Or you can stop tapping the pencil and get through to at least problem No. 8 on the worksheet because I know you can get at least that far, and if you choose to do that you'll only stay after school for two minutes. *It's your choice."* Then walk away.

Here's another thing to consider. If you're planning on writing a referral to a counselor or principal, you now have a specific, relevant situation to describe that will make you look very professional in the process. For instance, when you write down the exact steps you took in handling the situation, and you also write down the student's exact responses, do you see how reasonable you sound as a teacher? And do you see how defiant the student comes off in the face of your reasonable efforts? You make a great impression that way, and that can count for a lot with administrators.

The more evidence you have that you're taking the proper steps with this difficult student, the more you'll show your administrators that you're doing everything in your power to help *all* students learn.

BILL:
I see. I suppose if you make the punishment distasteful enough, you have a good chance of getting the student to come around.

TOM:
Yes, but don't rely on huge, negative "whammy" punishments. Make it reasonable and consistent. I mean, if he's the type of kid who jumps up at the sound of the bell and then runs out of the class with all this energy to be with his friends at lunch, then a punishment of just three minutes at lunch can be plenty effective. Don't take the whole lunch period. Just a few minutes. If that doesn't do the trick, then you can go to the next step, which could be an after-school detention or some other lunch detention where he gets his lunch brought to him but he has to eat alone.

There are lots of options there. Just go with punishments that you know you will do consistently and that your school will support.

BILL:
What else do you want to say about "Right Words?"

TOM:
You know what's fun about teaching? It's that your classroom is like your own real-life lab. I would say print the "Right Words" worksheet at the end of this chapter and tape it to your classroom desk. Then, every day try to put one into practice that particular day. When you use these — and I strongly urge you to use them right away — I want you to know one simple truth: they work! So use them until they become second nature.

The beauty of these techniques is being able to control any situation without it looking like you're trying to control anything. That's the beauty of "Right Words".

"RIGHT WORDS" WORKSHEET

Overview: Gaining control of confrontational situations with your students can be achieved by using "Right Words". As in many of the martial arts, the goal in using this strategy is to deflect and use the opponents' energy.

Here is a list of "Right Words" phrases:

1) Replace the word "frustrating" with "fascinating" or "interesting."

2) Say, "After listening to everyone's ideas, perhaps we should consider . . ." when introducing a suggestion to a skeptical person or group.

3) Use empathy linked to an action: "I know how you feel. I've felt that way before, and what I've found by trying _____ it helped things by _____.

4) As a last resort, end the meeting or walk away.

    4a) Say, "It doesn't seem we are going to solve this here, let's set an appointment with _____.
That's where these things get resolved."

5) "You know, I'd be happy to do _____. I'm only hesitant because (try to give positive reason here). Why don't we do (your suggestion) instead?"

6) Four possible responses to an inappropriate comment are:

    6a) Ask, "Why would you ask that?"

    6b) Ask "Why would you want to know that?"

    6c) Say, "You and I will talk about that later."

6d) Say, "That's not appropriate."

7) When needing to build consensus, preface your remarks by saying either:
- "I'm glad you said that . . ."
- "After listening to all of these ideas . . ."

8) When someone makes any accusation against you in front of a group, start your response by saying, "I'm glad you said that."

9) End with the phrase, "It's your choice" after explaining to a misbehaving student the benefits of returning to work versus the consequences that will occur if he continues to misbehave.

Points to remember from Chapter 6

▶ Kids have unlimited energy, so if you confront them day in and day out, you will lose at some significant level.

▶ Use "Right Words" to deflect the energy of students, parents and staff.

▶ Practice all ideas on the "Right Words" worksheet regularly.

▶ Pick one "Right Words" idea per day and see how you can put it to work.

▶ Print the "Right Words" worksheet and tape it to your classroom desk.

CHAPTER 7

Transforming students with 'Walk and Talk'

BILL:
Let's talk about Walk and Talk. What is it?

TOM:
It's my favorite strategy! Don't let the simplicity of this technique fool you. It allows you to have fun while improving your classroom instruction and managing students with ADHD. When you use Walk and Talk, you reconnect with all the reasons why you became a teacher. That in itself makes it a great strategy.

Walk and Talk is the single most effective way to transform your worst student into your best.

Walk and Talk, in a nutshell, is spending time each week walking and talking with students about anything at all. This establishes a one-on-one connection with an ADHD child — or any child — by simply walking with them to different places. There are opportunities during your day to take a student with you while you move about campus. For example, when you go to your school mailbox, you can ask a child to accompany you.

I'm talking about spending five to 10 minutes once a day. There's no hard and fast rule. If you do Walk and Talk whenever you can, the dividends will be huge.

BILL:
Why is this important?

TOM:
When people go on walks, they talk and act differently than they would in a class situation. It's a different dynamic. They open up and divulge more. Remember, for ADHD kids, there's no audience around on these walks. I cannot emphasize enough how valuable it is to talk with ADHD children without an audience to egg them on. For one thing, you are not in an adversarial position. In the classroom, you're face to face with students, telling them what to do. On a Walk and Talk, you're side by side sharing thoughts and ideas. Which scenario is going to be more effective with ADHD children?

BILL:
You mentioned taking a kid with you on your way to your school mailbox — where else could you go?

TOM:
Before we start, we need to discuss your obligation to the rest of the class. You must supervise your students. Never abandon your class to Walk and Talk with a student.

That being said, there are many ways to Walk and Talk with a student. You might use the first few minutes of your prep period, lunch, right before school starts, or right after the dismissal bell.

> *When people go on walks, they talk and act differently than they would in a class situation. And so it is with kids, too. It's a different dynamic. They open up and divulge more. I cannot emphasize enough how valuable it is to talk with ADHD children without an audience to egg them on.*

If you "team teach" with another teacher, the students are supervised when you leave the room for a quick Walk and Talk. You could line up a classroom guest speaker who

☼ Chalk Talk

I deeply believe in the Walk and Talk strategy. I used it with all my students; however, I made sure that the students who needed it the most would be the first to use it. I called it "chat time." Every day I would raffle the name of a person who would spend some private chat time with me. The kids loved the idea!

Dominique B., Lancaster, California

You wrote about taking walks and talking with your students and how this creates a different rapport between teacher and student. This truly does work! My students beg to walk with me. They open up and share what is in their hearts. It works like magic! Our relationship deepens and student behavior is positively affected.

Carolanne Z., St. Charles, Missouri

appreciates you taking an ADHD student on an errand, since it will make his presentation go a lot smoother. In elementary school, you could implement a "morning walk" program in which you Walk and Talk with a different student each day while supervising the rest of the class that is walking ahead of you.

I only use Walk and Talk in public areas around school to avoid appearances of impropriety. In fact, I'm never alone in the class with just one student, due to the litigious nature of our society.

Here's another example. Let's say you need to make copies. Bring along a student and do a Walk and Talk on the way. Maybe schedule a PE period — you can walk a lap around the track with a student. You can rotate taking different kids. That rotation method works especially well for elementary school teachers, or any teacher that has the same class all day long. You just rotate, focusing on different kids.

81

BILL:

Anything else?

TOM:

Yes. I write a general permission slip at the beginning of the school year that allows me to take my class to an adjacent park or to the library next door. As we walk, I walk 10 steps behind so I can supervise the entire class while talking with one child.

BILL:

Okay, so you've succeeded in getting a child to go on a walk with you . . . and then what? What do you talk about?

TOM:

I suggest you don't talk about school. **I want to be clear on this. You don't necessarily have to talk about *anything*.** It's just walking and listening and talking about life in general, or whatever

By walking with them and talking with my students I was able to achieve a much stronger relationship with them. Which, in turn, changed their classroom behavior dramatically. The one thing that I noticed was the students felt important and realized that I wanted them to do their best. I was able to communicate to them that I cared, and they let me know about what they needed to succeed in class.

Toni C., Denver, Colorado

Taking the time to get to know my students personally by "walking and talking" — to the office, to run an errand or anywhere — is quality, one-on-one time with a student that is priceless and shows the student you care and gives the teacher valuable knowledge that can be utilized in lesson planning. The kicker — it takes just minutes but the benefits will last the whole year!

Daphne I., Mercerville, New Jersey

happens to come up. It's relaxed and casual. It's a walk without any agenda whatsoever. The Walk and Talk achieves its goal whether you talk about something meaningful or not.

BILL:
Why is this important? What does this accomplish?

TOM:
It does a few important things. For one thing, *it breaks a pattern.* Your ADHD student has probably never walked and talked with any of his teachers before. If any previous teacher would have done Walk and Talk consistently with this student during any year in his life, this child probably would not still be disruptive. He'd likely be a completely different kid — for the better.

The beauty of this technique is that the child will tell you how to hook him into your class activities. Just by walking and talking, each kid will reveal ways you can work with him. He'll literally tell you what he needs and why he misbehaves. However, if you *try* to glean info from him during walks, it will work against you. The idea is to be relaxed, open, and simply "walk and talk."

The other critical aspect of Walk and Talk is that it prepares the ADHD child to follow directions before any crisis occurs where he must leave the classroom. I mean, think about it — for the first time in his life a teacher is asking him to join him in leaving the classroom and it *doesn't* involve him going to the principal's office!

That's significant in itself. The student is just walking and chatting about a movie he watched last night, what football team he likes, or his favorite music groups.

So when the ADHD student has an outburst, or there is a potential crisis where he must leave the classroom, he's accustomed to walking with you outside of class. He's more likely to follow your directions.

He's accustomed to walking with you, because he's done it plenty of times when his anxiety level was low. It's a positive association. So when his anxiety level rises and he's about to lose his temper, you ask him to go on a walk with you and he's likely to go.

☀ *Chalk Talk*

I taught a student who was reading and writing at a second-grade level. He was in his second year of fifth grade. He was labeled learning disabled and was a very bright, smart kid, but didn't channel his intelligence in the ways other students did. His classroom teacher had no management, which was an opportune time for Joe to act up, and get others in trouble. I used the Walk and Talk technique with him a lot and it was very effective. Also, I used the incentive survey with him and used it to develop behavior contracts with him. Thanks!

Jen C., Webster, New York

During a reading pull-out session one of my well-behaved students suddenly verbally attacked me. I sent her out of the room for the rest of the session. The next morning, I asked her homeroom teacher if the student could help me do some simple tasks. We ended up walking around for about an hour. We did not talk about the previous day at all. I thanked her for her help. That afternoon, during reading pull-out, she apologized to me without any prompting.

Wendy O., Chicago, Illinois

84

Remember, another benefit is that it demonstrates your dedication to your students.

I can tell you from personal experience that when you have an ADHD kid walking around with you on campus during lunch or prep time, the administration looks at you differently — and I mean that in a completely positive way. Their respect for you rises measurably. *Oh look, there's Mr. Daly, and he's walking and talking with the worst kid in school. He's actually* working *with Robert.*

Here's a tip: Do you want a tool to establish credibility on your campus as a teacher dedicated to your student's lives? Then, walk more often with your students. Always make sure your class is supervised and take a student when you leave the room. Do you need a cup of coffee down the hall? Take a kid and go. Do you need to make some copies in the office? Take a student along with you.

The opportunities are endless. Now, I'm not saying you bring a kid with you and have him break the copy machine in the teacher lounge, but he can help you in small tasks. Just remember, you're mainly interested in having him along for the walk.

You are establishing an important connection between you and the child. This can't be understated. When you make a real connection with an ADHD child, you greatly diminish the chance he'll end up in jail, jobless, or with any of the other problems that eventually plague some ADHD students. It often means the difference between a kid who falls on the wrong side of society's rules and a kid who lives a responsible, happy life.

Enlist support from everyone on campus. Think about the opportunities that present themselves. Say you're taking Jason on a Walk and Talk, and you run into Jim, the head landscaper. You introduce Jason and you spend just a minute or two talking to Jim about the new tree he's planting (or whatever it is he's doing that day). Pretty soon Jim is accustomed to seeing you walk around with Jason and before you know it Jim's saying, "Hey Jason, how ya doing? Check out this broken sprinkler head I'm working on."

People on campus will take a casual interest in your kids. All you
have to do is walk and talk and it will happen on its own. Believe
me, these little interactions add up to important personal connections
for Jason — it's the same thing you would do with your son, or a
nephew. You'd take him outside and your neighbors would get to
know him. Soon he'd feel like he was part of a community.

Bill, when you and I were kids, we knew our neighbors. There was
an inter-connectedness there; if those neighbors saw you do
something wrong, they'd let your parents know and you'd get in
trouble. I don't have to tell you that those days are gone. Not many
of us interact with our neighbors any more. Most of us don't even
know the people who live on our block.

Today, if you saw a kid on your street doing something wrong and
you tried to tell the parent about it, you'd probably be viewed
suspiciously. That's just the way it is now. That support system is
gone. So I think we need to offset that loss by creating a safety net
of support within the school.

By walking and talking with your ADHD student a couple of times per week, I guarantee that you will make a real, crucial connection with him within a matter of a few short weeks.

BILL:
What I like about this is that it's easy and natural.

TOM:
That's the beauty of Walk and Talk. As we know, when you go for a walk with someone, chatting is the most natural thing in the world to do. Walking is informal and casual. Spending "easy" time like that is one of the best ways to form a bond with a child. It takes you out of the classroom scenario.

How many people do we know with outdoor jobs? Many of those adults hated being stuck indoors in a classroom. Most of those adults coped with their schooling just fine, but kids with ADHD don't often possess the same emotional resources as everyone else. Walk and Talk is beneficial because they establish "anchoring experiences" that will help your students cope better in the classroom.

> *Being quiet shows the student that I'm not bringing him along for a heavy lecture, or trying to work an angle or soliciting information from him. This builds trust right away. Just the physical proximity of walking somewhere is enough for this to work.*

BILL:
Let's look at a specific example. Let's say I ask, "Okay, Kyle, when lunch starts, I have to get something from the science lab to bring back into class — can you help me out for five minutes?"

TOM:
That's a good example. Kyle is not upset or misbehaving at all. This is just a walk to the science lab. I might tell him, "C'mon, Kyle, let's go." He may respond, "Where are we going?" and I tell him, "We're just going to pick up something from the science lab."

After you do this a few times, Kyle won't even ask where you're going. He'll just join you, no questions asked because it's become an easy, natural thing.

So in this case, I might just explain, "I need a new science poster for our classroom," or whatever it is. But mostly what I'll do, at least during the first part of the walk, is not say anything at all. I may not say anything at all for a while.

Being quiet shows the student that I'm not bringing him along for a heavy lecture, or trying to work an angle or soliciting information from him. This builds trust right away. Just the physical proximity of walking somewhere is enough for this to work. Sometimes I might see something interesting, like a rabbit and point it out. It depends on where you are and the age of your student. Or, if I know the student will be receptive, I ask, "So, what did you do last night?" Often, the student will respond by talking about their favorite TV shows or music groups or what is going on with their friends.

BILL:
Sounds like it's not crucial what you say; it's only important to do this on a regular basis to establish a relationship, right?

TOM:
Exactly. If you're familiar with baseball, you know that the manager sometimes will visit the pitcher's mound to talk to his struggling pitcher. And sometimes the manager will go out there and say nothing at all! He's just going out there to check on the pitcher and just hang out with him for a moment as a way to see how he's doing.

Other times the manager will go out there and discuss where everyone is going out for dinner that night. I'm not kidding — that's really what happens sometimes. It's an effective technique. Walk and Talk offers the same sort of benefits.

BILL:
Can you give me a success story that involves Walk and Talk?

TOM:
There's too many to list. Every time I use it, it's effective. Every time I've used Walk and Talk with students, they tell me incredibly

88

useful things. Sometimes the conversations are about logistical stuff, such as a minor adjustment in their schedule. They'll actually tell you what they need. You don't need to root around or guess. They'll tell you straight-out what they need.

You'll discover things you would never find out in the classroom. You also hear what is most important to the student and his life.

TOM:
I want to point out something that's crucial: *All student misbehavior is an attempt to communicate something.* There's a communicative element to all forms of acting-out behavior.

So instead of the student feeling trapped in the classroom and tapping their pencil, or keeping his head down, or acting out in some way that's trying to communicate something, during a Walk and Talk the student will generally tell you what he needs in direct terms. That means you have a golden opportunity to end the misbehavior.

> *During a Walk and Talk, the student will generally tell you what he needs in direct terms. That means you have a golden opportunity to end the misbehavior.*

BILL:
How would you respond to a teacher who says, "Well, this sounds good, but I don't have time to walk with my students. In fact, I have no desire to walk anywhere with my kids, especially the ADHD ones!"

TOM:
I would tell that teacher that, number one: I appreciate your honesty. Number two: you're already wasting too much time by *reacting* to your students who are acting up. This technique will eliminate those behaviors before they occur, so it saves you time in the long run. And number three, you walk around campus anyway, so this strategy will simply weave into your day and doesn't have to add to your long "things to do" list.

BILL:
Are there any cautions to using this technique?

☼ Chalk Talk

This book had a tremendous impact on both my sanity and a particular third-grade student. It was my first year teaching, and I was given a young man who would throw huge tantrums where he would lay on the floor screaming and yelling. Anything from a tear in his paper or getting the wrong answer could set him off.

I had tried everything in my knowledge to deal with the problem: behavior chart, positive reinforcement, intervention from the principal and counselor; I even timed with a stopwatch how long he could go without whining or throwing a fit. He worked to improve his time each day. Nothing was working and I was frustrated, so I ran across the book on the Internet. It seemed to have all the answers, but I was skeptical. I ordered it because I had reached the last straw. The first part I read was about walking and talking with the student, but not forcing them to talk. At first, he was not very responsive, but I continued to talk with him before and after school.

Eventually, he started to open up and I began to see a little boy who had already been through more than I could even imagine. As a mutual respect began to develop, he truly wanted to make my day better and I wanted to help this struggling student whom I had grown attached to. We are nearing the end of the school year and I am still spending extra time with this student, not out of desperation, but because I truly enjoy his company. Thanks for the help!

Suzanne Vaira, third-grade, Las Vegas, Nevada

TOM:
Yes. You obviously need to be aware of any rules and procedures your school has about student-teacher interactions. **In this day and age, never be in a situation where your integrity and reputation could be put at risk. Just be aware of your school's policies and procedures, use your common sense, never leave your classroom unsupervised, and you'll be just fine.**

Points to remember from Chapter 7

► Walk and Talk is the single most effective way to transform your worst student into your best.

► Use Walk and Talk every day.

► When you use Walk and Talk, you will reconnect with all the reasons why you became a teacher.

► Walk and Talk succeeds, in part, because when people go on walks they talk and act differently than they would in a classroom situation.

► Remember that you don't have to talk about anything during a Walk and Talk.

► Walk and Talk is important because it breaks a pattern; it's likely that no other teacher has used Walk and Talk with your student.

► During a Walk and Talk, your student will literally tell you what he needs and why he misbehaves. However, don't actively try to glean information from him during walks, as it will work against you.

► If you want to bolster your credibility on campus as a dedicated teacher, try to avoid walking alone. Instead, take a student with you as often as you can.

► By using Walk and Talk with your student a couple of times per week, you will make a real, crucial connection with him within a few short weeks.

► Be aware of any rules and procedures your school has about student-teacher interactions. Never be in a situation where your integrity and reputation could be put at risk.

► Never leave the class unsupervised.

Teacher Quick Write #9

Where could I implement Walk and Talk
on my campus? _____

_____

_____

_____

_____

#10 Three times and situations I could Walk
and Talk with my students are

_____

_____

_____

CHAPTER 8

Interest Inventories: the secret door to your students' desires

BILL:
Let's talk about the "Interest Inventory."

TOM:
Interest Inventories are the perfect way to discover what really captures the attention of your students. They are a powerful tool in modifying the behavior of any child, as well as the best long-term tool you can use to plan your lessons, day in and day out.

BILL:
So Interest Inventories provide a roadmap for understanding what your students value, which in turn will show you a better way to implement lesson plans?

TOM:
Yes. They take the form of a fun survey that your students fill out, and you use the answers to gain a better understanding of your kids. **Interest Inventories tell you exactly what your kids want and need.** They provide a "hook" you will use to reach them through your lesson plans. That's an incredibly valuable tool for any teacher.

It illuminates the student's point of motivation, and it will drive your lesson planning.

BILL:
Why is that important?

TOM:
Well, for one thing, **it will prevent you from making wrong moves with your students.** Let me give you an example. Let's say you use stickers to reward students whenever they complete an assignment. And so you pick up some baseball stickers to pass out to the students. But it turns out that the student or students you're "rewarding" don't even like baseball. Maybe they're into football instead. So the stickers mean nothing to them. They would have worked twice as hard for the football stickers, but you don't have football stickers for them because you weren't aware of their true interests. That's just one small example.

Only use rewards that are effective motivating tools. For instance, once you find out which magazines and books your students read, you can pick those items up at garage sales, used bookstores, the Internet, from other teachers, and then use them as rewards. Kids will work hard to earn items they enjoy.

Here's the bottom line on Interest Inventories: If you find out what your students love, and you can gain access to the things they love, then you can modify their behavior. The teachers I've taught as my graduate students love them and continue to use them as invaluable tools.

The bottom line on Interest Inventories: If you find out what your students love, and you can gain access to the things they love, then you can modify their behavior.

BILL:
How about unstructured free time as a reward? Do you think that's a good idea?

TOM:
It's a bad idea in general, and it's a terrible idea with ADHD children. As we say, ADHD students *"don't do nothing well."* Think about that. They can't sit there and "do nothing." It's not something they're suited for. Never give ADHD kids completely unstructured free time.

Here's another solid reason to use Interest Inventories: **Many ADHD kids do not present themselves as being interested in anything.** You'll ask them, "Do you like this?" and they'll say, "No." *"Do you like that?" "No."* And on it goes. It feels like pulling teeth. It feels like the child is not interested in anything. But the Interest Inventory always succeeds in identifying at least a few things that interests each student.

BILL:
How do you implement it, exactly?

TOM:
It's easy to use. I administer it the first day of the class year. But you can use it any time of the year. Here's how it works: Directly ask your students what interests them by using written surveys. At the end of this chapter you'll find three versions of Interest Inventory surveys to use. The one entitled "Interest Inventory" is designed for children in seventh through 12th grade. It asks them a series of questions about their interests.

The kids shouldn't feel as if they're filling out some sort of official form or test. They're designed to be simple and fun. For example, one of the questions asks, "If you received four free tickets to the World Series, who would you take with you?" Another question asks, "If you could get free tickets to either the World Series, Super Bowl, Stanley Cup or NBA Finals, which would you choose?" Both of those questions will provide key information about what your student likes, along with the important people in his life, including his family.

You see, it's a way to learn about his support system without asking about his family directly. I wouldn't want to ask a kid about his family directly. That could be brutal for some kids who have parents in jail or live in foster homes, or don't even know their parents.

☀ *Chalk Talk*

In one of my older classrooms, I began by setting down the rules. I got all the students on my side by handing out one of the questionnaires. I got to know many of them through that questionnaire. They also asked me to fill one out so they could get to know me as well. I love your ideas. I only have my students for six weeks at a time, but I will always use the rules and questionnaires in every classroom from now on. Thanks for all your great ideas.

Lyne B., Boyle, Ireland

After teaching (or rather enduring) a particularly horrible Year-9 class which made me feel like I couldn't teach (and which led to me crying in frustration in the staff toilet) I used your Interest Inventory. I took them out of the free drama space and into a classroom where they sat and silently filled in the questionnaires. It opened up a host of "ways-in" for me. We like each other a lot now.

Jeanne S., Harlow, United Kingdom

BILL:
What do you do with the Interest Inventory surveys after the students fill them out? Take me through the actual process.

TOM:
You collect the sheets and go through them after school by making notes on a blank Interest Inventory. What I do is list all the students' answers and then make tally marks to track the frequency of certain responses. As you do this, certain responses will jump out at you, and you will use that information as jumping off points for your lessons.

BILL:
Can you give me an example?

96

TOM:

Sure. Let's say 80 percent of your kids like a certain music performer. You could write a sample of the performer's lyrics on the whiteboard, and then use those lyrics as a point of departure for beginning a discussion on your English lesson. That will more easily hook their attention than by just diving right into Chaucer. That's just one example. And, by the way, I want to point out that using these results doesn't *replace* your regular lesson plans, but they can enhance how you draw your students into the regular lesson materials.

The entire class will have fun with them. Here are a few more sample questions:

- *If you won a free shopping spree, what would you buy?*

- *If you could see anyone in concert, who would it be?*

- *If you could be anyone, who would it be?*

- *How would you describe yourself in four words?*

- *If you could study any animal on a safari, which would you choose?*

BILL:

Can you tell me a specific way in which you might use the survey results?

TOM:

Let's say you have a kid named Jimmy who can't sit still. Well, before you teach a life science class on bears you can pull him aside and say, "Hey, Jimmy, you said you were interested in bears. For a special project, I want you to jump on the Internet and get me some information on spectacled bears since our textbook is weak on that subject."

And so while the rest of the class is working on the regular class assignment, Jimmy does his special project and comes back with

97

information for the entire class. And so now Jimmy, who's been sort of an outcast because he's always acting out or in trouble because he can't stay on-task, is now a sort of hero. He's gone from heel to hero.

I promised before that you can transform your ADHD child into your best student. This is one of the ways.

BILL:
Let's back up a second. Jimmy is researching bears on the computer while the other kids are doing regular class work. Wouldn't the other kids gripe, "Hey, that's not fair. Why does Jimmy always use the computer?"

TOM:
Great point. You can have someone assist Jimmy with his special little project. Or even have two assistants. But the point is, you rotate his assistants among the other kids in the class. Maybe one assistant decides what to print out and another reports out to the class, but Jimmy runs the computer.

> *If you have ADHD kids in your class, you can't get around the fact that you need to do things a bit differently. That's just the way it is. You can't treat everyone exactly the same. You must be creative if you want them to succeed.*

BILL:
So you rotate the other student jobs in an equitable way?

TOM:
Yes. And you rotate Jimmy's job with the other two or three ADHD kids in class, too.

BILL:
But aren't those kids avoiding the regular class assignment?

TOM:
It's a tradeoff. They may not be doing the bookwork, but they are involved in powerful, problem-based learning.

BILL:
What's so powerful about it?

TOM:

Kids remember what they do more than what they hear. When those kids are asked at home, "What did you do learn about in school today?" those three kids won't hesitate at all in telling their parents about the spectacled bears. It will be memorable for them. Plus, you can *always* assign the regular assignment they missed in a modified version, either as in in-class assignment or homework.

BILL:

What are some other good effects of using the Interest Inventories?

TOM:

It enhances your class discussions and strengthens your connections with kids by proving that you're interested in them. Let me give you an example.

I taught a summer school class composed of ADHD children. These were kids who had spent time in residential psychiatric care and were slowly being reintroduced to the school system. My classroom was actually an experiment to see how these kids would fare on a comprehensive school site. And in using the Interest Inventory I discovered that all the kids in my class liked to eat cherries. So one day I saw cherries on sale and I picked up a three-pound bag and used them as a reward. For only $3.20, my class thought I was the best teacher they ever had.

BILL:

I'm sure any teacher could find opportunities like that.

TOM:

Oh sure. Recently I took my daughter on a weekend trip to Zion National Park in Utah. On the way back we stopped in a Las Vegas store and I ran across some items that had appeared on the answer sheets of my students' Interest Inventories.

So I picked up small items like stickers, magnets, and a class poster, and when I saw the class on Monday I handed out those items. You should have seen their faces! Even though the items were relatively small, the students were incredibly happy — and these students, like a lot of ADHD kids, are normally not happy about anything dealing with school and teachers.

BILL:
Wouldn't you need to buy stuff for all the kids to prevent resentment and favoritism?

TOM:
Yes, if it is not a performance-based reward, then you need to find something for everyone in the class.

BILL:
Isn't that expensive?

TOM:
It doesn't have to be. You'd be surprised. Another option is buying only one inexpensive thing that the entire class could use.

BILL:
Do you ever share the results of the surveys with your class?

TOM:
Yes, that's a great idea. It's fun for the students, especially if your class is a large one. For example, you can ask them, "Okay, what TV show do you think is the most popular one in this class?" It's fun for them to predict the results through a class discussion.

Let me give you another example of how this can work. I was a student teacher 19 years ago and in my class we had an ADHD kid who wasn't doing any school work. The lead teacher told me in private, "Okay, I'm handing the class over to you, but I don't expect you to do anything with Michael." Michael hadn't accomplished a single thing in this class.

BILL:
So what did you do with him?

TOM:
Well, I slipped him one of my earliest versions of the Interest Inventory. He wasn't doing the regular class work anyway, so I gave him a survey to fill out while everyone else was doing the regular

☼ *Chalk Talk*

I had a student who was more of the HYPOactive rather than the HYPERactive. I figured that if I gained his interest or his respect he was more likely to do his work. Through Interest Inventories and simple Walk and Talks, I found out he was into skateboarding. So naturally I filled him in how I used to be a skateboarder as well. We discussed a few types of tricks and whether either of us could do them. I told him I could "ollie" which is the basic skateboarding trick to jump the board off the ground.

A few days later he brought in his skateboard for whatever reason. Later that day I was sitting at my desk grading papers when I happened to notice this student pacing back and forth in front of my desk.

I knew he was up to something but what I wasn't sure. After about 10 paces he finally stopped, looked straight at me and said, "Mr. Spears, I want to see you "ollie"! This was great! I could tell he wanted to say something. He was building up the courage to do so — and he did! I said, "Well, I'll tell you what, you're lucky. I wore my tennis shoes today!" So I "ollied" for him. He was blown away — you should have seen his jaw hit the ground. He couldn't believe it! A teacher that could "ollie"!

From that day on he began to slowly build trust in me and began to open up. After that he would do things like pull his chair up to my desk and ask to chat, or most of the time he would have his own topic---usually politics! The point being that once I made that connection he was eager to do what he needed to do and would initiate activities on his own rather than being withdrawn and isolating himself.

He passed with flying colors this year and I vividly remember him leaving the school with a smile!

Shawn S., Ohio

101

assignment. Through his completed survey, I found out he was into Mustang cars. No one thought this kid had an interest of *any* kind, but it was obvious from his answers on the Interest Inventory that he was crazy for Mustangs.

BILL:
So what did you do with that information?

TOM:
During the next few days I bought two Mustang magazines. I sat down and thought about what I could do with these magazines.

BILL:
What did you come up with?

TOM:
Well, I took a sheet of paper and wrote three questions on it, one at the top, one in the middle, and one toward the bottom. The first question said, "Describe the Mustang on Page 42." The next one asked, "If you could buy any Mustang in this magazine, which one would you buy, and why." And the last question was, "Compare any two Mustangs in this magazine." And let me tell you, he didn't leave a single line of white space on that sheet of paper. He filled out the whole thing. And this was a kid who wouldn't complete anything in school.

BILL:
Wait — that's not fair that everyone else in the class is taking a test and this kid is sitting there with a Mustang magazine, is it?

TOM:
If you have ADHD kids in your class, you can't get around the fact that you need to do things a bit differently. That's just the way it is. You can't treat everyone exactly the same. You must be creative if you want them to succeed.

And that also means being firm about what you have to do. Your other students will respect that. I had an eighth-grade kid say to me, "That's not fair." And I told him, "Jeffrey, I'll tell you what — when you get your teaching credential, we'll discuss doing it your way. For now, you need to focus on your job and let me take care of Michael. That's the deal."

BILL:
What else could you do in this situation?

TOM:
Well, let's say you set up a class reward for a pre-determined amount of total class on-task time. And let's say the reward is a pizza party. And Michael is always off-task and that is killing the class' chance for the pizza party . . .

BILL:
So you count Michael's Mustang work as "on-task"?

TOM:
Well, not exactly in those words, but you can use that as leverage for getting the support of someone like Jeffrey. You can say to him, "Hey, we're not on pace for making the pizza party. I need to try something different to get Michael working."

BILL:
And asking Jeffrey what kind of pizza he likes might quash his complaint.

TOM:
Exactly. I have two words to say on this issue of letting Michael use the Mustang magazine while other kids took a test: *It worked!* The first day he did the magazine and the other kids worked. But the second day, when I gave the kids a worksheet based on Gettysburg, I handed Michael the top half of the Gettysburg worksheet. I told him that if he finished the top half, without rushing through it, that he could take home the Mustang magazine.

On Day 3, he finished the entire regular class assignment for the reward of reading the magazine. So within three days I had him completely on-task, doing all the class work — all based on information that was originally gleaned through the Interest Inventory.

BILL:
Anything else you want to say about the Interest Inventory?

TOM:
Well, just this — a lot of the questions are specifically designed for a purpose even though many of them will seem random. But they reveal crucial information. For instance, consider question No. 5, "What's the best concert you ever attended?" We ask that question for specific reasons. It's a way to find out what values and rules are set by the family at home. If a sixth-grader puts down that he's been to all sorts of concerts by himself, he's either a liar or maybe there's no one at home setting boundaries for him.

Or, using the opposite end of this example, what if a 12th grader writes that he's *never* been to an amusement park? That might indicate that either he can't afford to go or that his family may not allow him to go.

Another good example of using the survey is question No. 7 asking about previous school projects the student has completed. The student's answer can prevent you from duplicating an assignment, or it could assist you in building further on an interest they have already developed.

Teacher Quick Write #11

The survey most appropriate for my class is (look over the surveys at the end of this chapter) _____

#12 Modifications I may need to make to the survey I plan to use are _____

#13 Ways I plan to use the information gleaned from the surveys are _____

► Interest Inventories tell you exactly what kids want and need. This will allow you to:

- Modify the behavior of all students.
- Create meaningful class rewards.
- Write dynamic lesson plans.
- Involve kids who would rather sleep in class.
- Treat kids differently based on their needs.
- Demonstrate that you are focused on your students.

► There are three surveys to choose from; select the right one for your class.

► Administer the surveys, tally the results and discuss results in class.

► When discussing results, be careful not to embarrass a student.

► Administer the surveys two times a year to keep up with your students' interests.

INTEREST INVENTORY FORMS

Overview: The following three surveys are highly useful teaching aides that you can implement during your very first day in class. As perhaps the most practical and helpful exercises in this book, the information gained from these pages will provide a teaching advantage that will last the entire school year.

Rationale: The Interest Inventory stems from "Grandma's Rule," which is something we've all heard: that you have to eat your peas before you can have dessert. Formally developed in the 1970s by UCLA researcher David Premack, this exercise operates from the principle that if you discover the things your students enjoy, then you can more easily modify their behavior. How is this possible? By making a fun activity contingent upon his completion of a required task that may not be as fun.

Although we may think we know what kids like, we need to use an Interest Inventory to determine a student's own reinforcement hierarchy. This is exactly what these three surveys are designed to do.

The benefits of "Premack's Principle" are three-fold:
1.   By directly asking your students what truly fascinates them, you will discover critical "inside information" that you will use as a pivotal part of your classroom management plan.

2.   In building upon the interests of your students, you will effectively implement specific lesson plans and make learning come alive with fun and purpose. For example, if it turns out that many students in your class are fans of, say, the Philadelphia Eagles, then you might use football analogies in solving a math problem.

3.   By taking the time to find out what interests your students, you will establish an invaluable connection that instantly creates rapport, goodwill, and trust. As the adage states, "No one cares about how much you know until they know how much you care."

How to use: To maximize the benefit of these surveys, do them early in the year — as early as the first class. Simply make photocopies of the Interest Inventory, and have students fill in their answers during class. Collect their sheets and then tally the responses on your own after class. Make notes as to which subjects are most frequently listed. Then, during the next day's class, have fun with your class in discussing the results. Ask them questions such as, "Okay, guys, what do you think the class's favorite music group is?" Also, I recommend giving the surveys out a second time halfway through the school year because kid's interest are always changing!

Finally, if a new student is added to your class during the course of the year, give him the Interest Inventory right away. This will make him feel a welcomed part of the class, and you will get a quick read on where he is coming from.

Note: Each of the following three surveys are designed for varying ages. The Interest Inventory is for fourth through 12th graders. The Reinforcement Survey, which may need to be read aloud to the class, should be used for kindergarten through grade four. All About You can be used for grades two through seven. However, use your own discretion in selecting an interest survey for your particular class.

INTEREST INVENTORY   <u>Name</u>_____

1) What are your favorite TV shows?

2) What movies do you like that are now on DVD or VHS?

3) Which movies have you recently seen at the theater that you liked?

4) What are some of your favorite songs? Music videos?

5) What are your favorite music groups? What types of music do you like best?

6) Have you ever been to a concert? What's the best concert you ever attended?

7) Who would you like to see perform in concert?

8) What's the best amusement park you ever visited? What is your favorite ride?

9) What was the school project you found the most fun last year?

10) Have you ever met someone famous? Did they give a speech?

11) If you could meet anyone in the world, who would it be?

12) If you could be any animal, which would it be? Why?

13) If you could go on safari and study any animal, which would it be?

14) What is your dream career?

15) If you could be anyone for a day, who would it be?

16) Do you know how to dance?

17) What do you do in your free time?

18) What magazines do you like to read?

19) If you could buy any three books, which books would you buy?

20) What type of novels do you like — romance, mystery, or some other type?

21) What are your favorite stores at the mall?

22) If you won a free 30-minute shopping spree in a mall, what would you fill your shopping cart with?

23) Do you watch WWF? If so, who are your favorite wrestlers? Who are your least favorite?

24) Do you have a computer and printer at home? Does it have Internet access?

25) What do you know how to do on the computer?

26) What is your favorite thing to do with a computer?

27) What are your favorite web sites? How much time per week do you spend surfing the Web?

28) What was the best field trip you ever went on?

29) What places have you visited? What were your favorite places?

30) Have you ever been camping? If so, where? What did you like about it?

31) Where would you like to go camping?

32) What are your favorite sports to play? What position?

33) Is there any sport you are interested in learning?

34) You are told you have five free tickets to either the Super Bowl, the World Series, the NBA Finals, or a WWF title match. Which would you choose and who would you take?

35) What are your favorite sports to watch on TV? Live?

36) What are your favorite teams?

       Team   Players

  Basketball:
  Baseball:
  Football:

37) What team sports have you played?

38) What are your favorite foods for dinner and lunch?

39) What are your favorite fruits and vegetables?

40) What are your favorite snack foods?

41) Are you a vegetarian? Are there any foods that you are not allowed to eat?

REINFORCEMENT SURVEY

For each of the following items, tell whether you would like to receive and/or participate in each item as follows:

1 = Not Interested 2 = Interested 3 = Very Interested

__Cookie	__Potato chips	__Chew Gum
__Soda pop	__Candy bar	__Popcorn
__Stickers	__Baseball Cards	__Play Checkers
__Work puzzle	__Read a Book	__Behavior Certificate
__Computer game	__15 min. free time	__Write on Chalkboard
__Sidewalk Chalk	__Time to draw / color	__Talking to friend
__Video for Class	__Teacher's Helper	__Taking care of class pet
__Lunch with the	__Listening to music	__Make an announcement
__Principal	__Pretzels	__Cheetos
__Cheese-its	__Other	

_____

List 3 favorite things to do:
1.
2.
3.

List 3 favorite things to eat or drink:
1.
2.
3.

What are your favorite sports?
1.
2.
3.

What are your favorite TV shows or cartoons?
1.
2.
3.

ALL ABOUT YOU!

Name_____

1. What are your favorite TV shows?

2. What are your favorite movies or videos?

3. What are your favorite songs?

4. What are your favorite music groups?

5. Do you have any pets? What are their names?

6. What is your favorite food for breakfast, lunch or dinner?

7. What are your favorite colors?

8. What are your favorite candies?

9. What are your favorite fruits or vegetables?

10. If you could be any animal in the world, which would you choose?

11. What is your favorite sport to watch or play?

12. What is your favorite season and why?

CHAPTER 9

The win-win way to show movies in your classroom

BILL:
I understand there's an effective way to utilize movies in the classroom.

TOM:
Yes. What I'd like to discuss is how to use movies to demonstrate that you are an outstanding teacher.

BILL:
I suppose it's easy for a parent to view the showing of movies in the classroom as a teacher's easy way out?

TOM:
Yes. I want you to imagine the following scenario. You're working as a teacher, and you've selected a movie that is relevant for your kids. And as you're showing the movie, the principal drops in unannounced and says in a suspicious tone of voice, "Oh, you're showing a *movie again!*"

Some teachers would be nervous in this situation for fear that it makes them look less professional. Kids, after all, *watch movies at home. You should be teaching!* But here's a method where you will look like a true professional every time you show a movie.

BILL:
How do you do that, exactly?

TOM:
By using a "Movie Worksheet." There are two steps. Number one, make sure the movie you're showing is relevant. For example, I've shown "Osmosis Jones," an animated movie with Chris Rock that shows the circulatory system, red and white blood cells, and great human anatomy. It's a terrific movie and the kids were really into it. I've also shown "Medicine Man," and "Dante's Peak" for earth science, and there are many movies you can show relative to English/language arts that build vocabulary.

So, number one, find a movie that fits in with what you're teaching.

Next, watch the movie a couple times on your own before showing it to your class. That way, you'll determine if it's appropriate for your class. You'll also develop a set of questions from watching the movie. And having these questions will set you apart from the misguided perception that you're simply showing a movie out of laziness.

BILL:
What type of questions are you developing?

TOM:
You will develop three types of questions:

- Pre-movie
- During the movie
- Post-movie

The first type of questions you'll assemble are questions that the kids will be answering *before* they view the movie. It's called the "Vocabulary Worksheet." The Vocabulary Worksheet is a list of words from that particular movie that the kids should know before the movie even starts. It is not just dictionary-type vocabulary, but also figures of speech, colloquialisms and commonly used phrases that many students might not understand.

For example, I showed a movie called "Jimmy Neutron Boy Genius" and on my Vocabulary Worksheet was the phrase "butter up," because that's an example of a phrase that many of my students didn't know.

As the movie is being shown, students complete the second part of the movie sheet with **comprehension questions** on it. These are questions you assembled while watching the movie on your own beforehand. These comprehension questions periodically arise throughout the movie.

The comprehension questions are designed to make students think while they watch the movie. But it is okay to ask a few easy questions just to ensure they're paying attention to the movie details.

For example, I show a movie called "October Sky." It's an excellent movie about kids from a coal-mining town who built rockets. One of my questions for that movie is, "What is the name of the town where the coal mine is located?" That's an example of a simple question to make sure the kids are paying attention. A more thinking-type question is, "Why do you think Homer felt bad when his Dad yelled at him?"

> *I highly recommend you send the list of movies you plan to show to all parents with the welcome-back letter during the first week of school.*

BILL:
Okay, so the kids have already completed the Vocabulary Worksheet before the movie, and as the movie is rolling they're answering the comprehension questions on a sheet right in front of them?

TOM:
Right. And now let's return to the scenario in which your principal walks into the room. She sees your students watching a movie, but you're not worried in the least because you hand her a copy of your worksheet. Right at that point might be a good time to tell your class, "Okay, kids, question number eight is coming up, pay attention," and, now, instead of a skeptical principal you have an impressed administrator who will walk out of your class with a smile

on her face, a copy of your movie worksheet in her hands, and a favorable impression of you.

Very often the principal will ask you two things:

    (1) "Can I keep this?"

    (2) "Can I share this with the other teachers?"

It makes a great impression. It's best if you can watch the movie with your students, sitting near your ADHD students. But in a time squeeze, it's also an opportunity for you to work while the movie is being shown. For instance, you can do some grading, or some other miscellaneous tasks. Just make sure you are sitting near the disruptive kids to keep them on-task. Bottom line is, there's nothing wrong with showing a movie twice a month, as long as you do it this way.

BILL:
What do you do when the movie ends?

TOM:
That's where you use the **expansion questions**. This is the section of the worksheet with follow-up questions. An example might be, "How does Homer's town compare with our city today?" You make the movie a more meaningful experience.

The worksheets will improve attentiveness during the movie. It keeps them focused, and they're less likely to put their heads down or act up. **Once again, it's a good idea to sit near your ADHD kids during the start of the movie** — just quietly sit between your two worst kids and point out some of the questions. That will keep the ADHD kids on-task. Plus, your viewing of the movie with them is good role modeling for the rest of the class.

BILL:
What are some other benefits to showing a movie in this way?

TOM:
Well, once you have established a number of different movies that you show in a school year, and you develop the worksheets to go

☀ *Chalk Talk*

When I first saw that you had sent me Movie Notes, I never dreamed that I would be able to use them with pre-K children. However, the questions for "Finding Nemo" were great! My students really had to think, and since recalling details is one of our goals before they move on to kindergarten, it was an excellent way to get them to recall facts! Thank you very much!

Becky W. Louisville, Kentucky

I used your Movie Notes with my preparations for showing "The Little Rascals" and my students responded to the handout that I took from your book. It was one of the best moments I had with my students.

Mary Lou K., Tarzana, California

Using the movies as actual lessons has been great; I'd always felt guilty showing a video but you've proved how effective that can be.

Debbie C., Maryborough, Australia

along with those movies, **you now have 20 hours of legitimate lesson plans ready to roll.** And it's actually fun to watch the movies beforehand and prepare the worksheet!

These ready-to-go lesson plans will be utilized when an emergency comes up. If you unexpectedly need to leave the classroom and another adult is going to supervise your kids — well, now you have a movie to show them, but it's not just a movie, it's a legitimate learning experience.

Also, the movie is a treat, and the kids will work to earn the privilege of seeing a great movie. Set up the movie as both a reward and a learning experience. Tell the kids at the beginning of the school year that you have 10 movies approved for classroom showing, and that you will show them if certain expectations are met.

I recommend telling the principal beforehand. Tell her that you'll be showing a maximum of one movie per month, but that you'll only be showing each film as long as your students meet some specific goals. This way, the students will know that you and the principal are working together, and the principal will appreciate knowing the rationale and benefit behind the movies. **I also highly recommend you send the list of movies to all parents with the welcome-back letter during the first week of school.**

Now, for a great, advanced technique, use the Interest Inventory to find out which movies the ADHD students really love and then work out an individual contract with the student (or students) that effectively says, "We'll show your movie next week, but this is what we need to do first."

Remember to make the goal something that the students can realistically accomplish. Set a reachable goal. Once the students meet the goal, you might acknowledge those kids to the rest of the class this way: "We are seeing this movie today because, as a class, we were on-task 95 percent of the time. And I want to especially point out how much Billy, Justin and Tamara improved as a great example to the whole class."

BILL:
Any cautions to using the movie worksheets?

TOM:
The first caution is to not overuse this. I would not show a movie once a week. Our kids are far enough behind as it is. Don't make it worse by showing movies all the time. So I would say twice a month, at the most.

The other caution is to never show an R-rated movie. The exception might be if you've been teaching U.S. history in high school for many years and you have specific parental permission to show something like "Schindler's List," "Glory," or "The Patriot." In those cases, with specific permission from your principal, it might be okay. But I would personally never show R-rated movies under any circumstances, even if all my students were 17 and 18 years old. Older kids will beg for R-rated movies but I always tell them I won't do it.

Here's a great way to protect yourself: Before hosting the fall open house, write an introductory letter home to parents, and let them know which movies you're planning to show throughout the year. Tell them you'll be at the open house an hour early so that if any parents are concerned about any of the planned films, they can preview a movie in your classroom before the open house.

Print an approval form that says, "If you do not want your child watching any of these movies, please list which ones they are and return this sheet to me." By informing parents what movies you're going to show, sending home a form in which they can opt out of specific movies for their kids, and allowing them a chance to preview the movies, any parental complaints to the principal will be refuted by the letter. You'll demonstrate that you took necessary precautions.

We happened to be at the end of reading "The Mouse and the Motorcycle" when I received your Movie Notes, and I promptly used it that week! The kids thought it was great and they did a good job on the questions.

Brenda B., third grade, Camanche, Iowa

Your Movie Notes helped me turn video time into productive learning time!

Janice M., San Diego, California

Points to remember from Chapter 9

▶ There are three parts to all good movie worksheets: Vocabulary, Comprehension and Expansion.

▶ Teach three to five vocabulary words a day prior to the movie.

▶ Use comprehension questions during the movie to ensure that students are following the action.

▶ After the movie, ask expansion questions and create expansion activities.

▶ Always do the following:

- Preview the movie and ask yourself, "Is this appropriate?"
- Send parents a list of movies you plan to show that year.
- Develop 10 movie worksheets each summer before school starts.
- Sit between your ADHD kids when watching the movie.
- Show only one or two movies a month.

MOVIE WORKSHEET: An Introduction

Overview: Most teachers use movies to supplement their classroom instruction. However, my corollary to Murphy's Law is that the day you show your students a movie, the vice principal stops by to evaluate your instructional practices. Imagine the look on her face when she observes each student grossly involved in a meaningful movie because of an effective worksheet you created that turned an otherwise empty viewing experience into a powerful, unforgettable learning exercise!

How to use: The following Teacher Worksheet is designed for the teacher to use while viewing the movie at home. There are three sections to the Student Movie Worksheet: Vocabulary, Comprehension, and Expansion.

1. "Pre-teach" the Vocabulary section the days before showing the movie in class. **Best practice: teach three to five vocabulary words a day for three days prior to the movie.** Always take the time to really discuss the vocabulary words with the class as a group. Talk them through the hard to pronounce words and make the vocabulary come alive!

2. During the movie, students follow the action by answering comprehension questions.

3. After the movie, students reflect on it by responding to the expansion questions.

Teacher Worksheet

Title: _____   Run time: _____

Rating: _____   Suggested grade level:_____

Vocabulary: List 5 to 15 vocabulary words from the movie. If the movie is to be shown on a Friday, teach five words per day on Tuesday, Wednesday and Thursday.

1	6	11
2	7	12
3	8	13
4	9	14
5	10	15

Main characters, relationships, character types, or major actors:

Plot questions: What is the story about? Questions about the storyline.

Suggestions for follow-up activities in groups or pairs: Activities or projects that reinforce some event or vocabulary from the movie.

1. Art projects   4. Other group projects
2. Sports projects
3. Crosswords/puzzles

Suggestions for stop times: Do you want to stop the movie and discuss issues? Where should you stop the movie? What should be discussed?

Prediction questions: What do you think will happen next?

Suggested books, articles or readings:

    1.   Find related articles on the Internet.

    2.   Find related topics in your textbooks.

Suggested follow-up individual activities:

Comprehension questions: List questions to ask students while the movie is being shown. Suggestion: Ask a question to ask every 5 to 10 minutes.

1.

2.

3

4.

5.

6.

7.

8.

9.

Expansion Questions: What questions do you want students to answer after the movie? Hint: Use questions with phrases such as, *Compare it to, Describe, Tell me more about, What would you do, What did you like most and What would you change.*

1.

2.

3.

4.

5.

6.

7.

8.

9.

10.

STUDENT MOVIE WORKSHEET

October Sky   Name _____ Date _____

Vocabulary:

1. launch	8. satellite	15. orbit
2. milestone	9. Soviet	16. Cold War
3. soar	10. rocket	17. coal
4. cylinder	11. Sputnik	18. shaft
5. miner	12. weld	19. combust
6. union	13. strike	
7. evaporate	14. dilute	

Comprehension questions:

1.   What was the name of the town in the movie?

2.   What kind of industry supported the town?

3.   What event influenced Homer's decision to study rockets?

4.   Who first invented rocketry?

5.   Where did they get their materials to build their rockets?

6.   Where did they go to test their rockets and why?

7.   What happened when they first launched their rockets?

8.   Why did they stop building rockets?

9.   Why did Homer volunteer to work in the coal mine?

10.   Why did he decide to return to building rockets?

11.   Why did Homer go to Indiana?

12.   What did Homer win in Indiana?

13.   What did Homer end up doing for a living?

Expansion questions:

1.   Compare and contrast where Homer lives to where we live.

2.   Do you think the boys were good friends? Tell why.

3.   In what ways did the teacher motivate the boys?

4.   Explain some of the differences between Homer's mother and father.

5.   Homer decided to quit school and work in the coal mine. What would you have done in that situation? Why?

6.   If you could become an expert in something, what would you choose and why?

7.   Homer followed his dream. What is your dream? How will you make your dream a reality?

CHAPTER 10

How to use journals to improve your students' writing skills

TOM:
Our children don't write enough in school. Let me paint a scenario in regard to how teachers commonly use journal writing, and then I'll show you an easy technique to revolutionize this activity.

In the usual method, the teacher picks a journal topic for the day and writes it on the board. And let's say you're an ADHD child and you have a lot going on in your head. You have a difficult home environment, you're on medication, and you had a rough morning. And so you hurry into class only to find that the teacher has once again written on the blackboard a stupid topic for journal writing.

In fact, the topic may even be one that the teacher already used last month. And think of the overworked teacher — she may be tired, frazzled, and thinking, "Okay, the bell is ringing in 30 seconds and I need to pick *another* topic of the day." It's just another stress for her, and on top of that Billy is complaining that the class already did that topic last month, or that he hates this topic, and before you know it there is an argument that leads to her writing a referral that sends Billy to the office. It sets up a no-win power struggle.

Here's the better way to do it. Let each student have his or her own writing journal that stays in the classroom. It doesn't have to be anything fancy. It could be a 70-page spiral notebook. In the back of that journal you staple or glue a series of topics for the kids to select.

The one I use has 50 journal topics (at the end of this chapter). So every day when it's journal writing time, I say to the kids, "It's journal writing time," and they simply open up to the back of their journal and find a topic that interests them on that particular day. Studies show that if students choose their own assignment, they are more likely to complete the work and succeed because you gave them the choice.

So look at what you've done — you've eliminated the power struggle. You've eliminated the whining and complaining. You've eliminated the stress of creating new and original topics every day. And now all you do is simply walk around the room to make sure everyone has selected a topic and has started writing.

> *So look at what you've done — you've eliminated the power struggle. You've eliminated the whining and complaining. You've eliminated the stress of creating new and original topics every day. And now all you do is simply walk around the room to make sure everyone has selected a topic and has started writing.*

BILL:
What are the benefits of journal writing for these kids?

TOM:
The main benefit of journal writing is the academic engagement of the student. One of the worst things that can happen to ADHD students is that they get older without learning anything. So what journal writing does is engage the student in a topic he enjoys.

BILL:
Is this something you recommend doing every day?

TOM:
Yes, every day, for 20 minutes. It's a great thing. And during that time I monitor the kids, and sometimes I even model this behavior by

sitting next to the most pronounced ADHD child and writing in my own journal. If you have two ADHD kids who sit near each other,

Chalk Talk

I was impressed with the Journal Topics. The students were agreeable to doing the writing at the beginning of the class period since they had a choice of topics. Plus, the students were happy to express opinions about "taboo" subjects such as violence, stealing, and school improvement.

Jaynee S., Belle, West Virginia

Writing journals has been very successful for my students. They call them "sharing books." The students like the freedom to write about what they wish, but they appreciate having the topics listed inside their books.

Marcia M., Victoria, British Columbia, Canada

It showed me that if I allowed the student to write on a topic of interest to them, they would write and actually enjoy doing this task.

Judy D., Trumann, Arkansas

you can sit between them. That works great.

And here's an interesting benefit: When parents attend open house, or a parent-teacher conference, the students' journals are one of the most compelling points of interest for the parents. When they see what topics their own kids selected, and then they read what they've written, the parents gain a better appreciation for the accumulation of learning that's taken place in your classroom.

Anyone who doubts your instructional practices can simply open up these journals. Do you have any idea how many pages begin stacking up when you're writing for 20 minutes a day? It's huge. Parents will gain a new appreciation for their children, too.

However, you really should tell your students that their parents have the right to read their journals. Generally, this is more of an issue for students in grades 5 to 12.

Here is a modification that some of my teachers use to protect their students' privacy: If a student writes something personal that she does not want the teacher to share with others, she simply dog-ears that page in her journal. The teacher then must remember to remove those pages before sharing the student journals with other adults.

BILL:
So you keep the journals in the classroom? The kids don't take them home and bring them into class each day?

TOM:
No, the journals must stay in classroom! Otherwise, someone will always be leaving his at home. A smart way to do it is to have the journals already sitting on the kids' desks when they arrive.

BILL:
Do you recommend journal writing at the beginning of the class or at the end?

TOM:
I usually do it toward the beginning, but I don't think it matters. It just depends on what works best for you.

BILL:
Where can readers find a list of topics?

TOM:
We listed sample topics in the back of this book. I also want to point out that the topics cover a broad range of subjects. Science, history, English, social studies, and social skills development — the topics run the gamut because writing across the curriculum is important.

Just print out the list, then glue or staple the list to the inside of the back covers of your journals.

Points to remember from Chapter 10

► Journal writing is a great way to engage children in topics they love while developing their writing skills.

► Let each student have his or her own writing journal that stays in the classroom.

► Staple or glue a series of topics to the inside of the back cover of each journal.

► If students select their own writing topics, they are more likely to complete the work and succeed. So the students are allowed to either select a topic from the list, or do their own creative writing based on what is on their minds that morning.

► Have your students write in their journals every day for 20 minutes. Consider modeling by sitting next to the most pronounced ADHD child and writing in your own journal. If you have two ADHD kids who sit near each other, sit between them.

Journal Topics For Students:

Worksheets

Overview:
Use journal writing to stimulate the excitement of learning. An easy and effective way to incorporate this activity: Instead of introducing a new journal topic each day, simply place the following list of topics in your students' journals. This way, they can view the list as they would a menu and select the topic that interests them most on any particular day. This will increase their ongoing participation. Print out the list and staple it to the inside of each student's journal. Instruct your students to write the date next to each entry they selected to keep them accountable. Or, create a separate writing log for students to record their writing.

Name _____

Date Completed

_____ List 20 things you and your friends do for fun.

_____ Describe your favorite five foods to eat around the holidays.

_____ Write about rain. When were you drenched by rain? Where
are fun places to be during the rain? Have you seen rain cause accidents?

_____ Go back in time four years. Describe your playthings and friends.
Write a letter to that person you were eight years ago.

_____ Do you think boys or girls have it easier? Why?

_____ Imagine that you can travel all over the USA. Where will you go
and what will you do there for fun?

_____ Have you ever used violence? Describe what happened.

_____ Contemplate your future after you graduate from high school. Where
will you live? What job will you have? What will you do for fun?

_____ List four jobs you might want to have as an adult and discuss why.

_____ Write in detail about your dream car. Describe everything about it.

_____ Describe two interesting places you have visited.

_____ Describe three of your favorite movies.

_____ Explain what harassment means to you, and give three examples.

_____Do you think you have too many chores? If you could assign the
chores in your house, which ones would you take for yourself?

_____Detail five things you could do to increase your grades.

_____ What accomplishment makes you most proud and why?

_____ Contemplate the world's future 10 years from now. What new inventions will we have? What will people eat? Will the world be safer?

_____ Describe in detail the worst car you have ever been inside.

_____ Write anything you want about fish. Ideas might include fishing trips, Sea World visits and fish tanks you've seen.

_____Give five examples of using good manners and being polite.

_____List 20 compliments to give someone that are not about their looks.

_____Discuss five things you are thankful for this year.

_____ What foreign country would you like to visit most?   Why?

_____Name seven appropriate and inexpensive places to go on a date.

_____ Write five good reasons why it is not okay to hit other people. Write about a time when you were hurt or in pain.

_____What is the funniest movie you ever saw?

_____When mad at someone, what are five things to do to avoid violence?

_____Describe four jobs you'd enjoy working while in high school.

_____Describe the scariest movie you ever saw.

_____What could you do to improve the quality of your teachers?

_____List three times you did not follow a staff member's directions.

_____ If you were a scientist, what diseases would you try to cure? Also, list five diseases and explain what you know about them.

_____ Describe your least favorite foods to eat around the holidays.

_____ What are five ways to avoid arguing in order to solve conflicts peacefully?

_____Describe a time when you were in the snow. If you've never been in the snow, describe a time when you were cold.

_____Discuss your favorite animals, or animals you do not like.

_____Write about a time when someone made you feel better when you were feeling down.

_____List five things you do in school to get along with others.

_____List five good reasons why a person should want to learn in school.

_____Describe four to six different animals in detail.

_____Write about your best and worst birthdays.

_____What should you do to prepare for an earthquake?

_____Describe the following items to a friendly alien from Planet X: The wind, the snow, a racecar, a sporting event, and a mountain.

_____ Are there any types of stealing or borrowing without permission that you feel is acceptable? Explain.

_____ Describe the saddest movie you ever saw.

_____What are three of the biggest differences between what happens on TV and what happens in the real world?

_____Describe a time when someone gave you a lack of respect. Explain three ways to show respect to others.

_____ Analyze what characteristics make a good parent.

_____What things do your parents tell you that you find hard to believe?

_____Explain a time when you fixed something. How did you fix it? Do you like fixing things? Why or why not?

CHAPTER 11

Getting your students to see the bigger picture with 'The Stoplight'

BILL:
What do you do about a child who is being defiant? He's saying, "I'm not going to do that," or "You can't make me do that."

TOM:
A teacher cannot physically *make* a student pick up his pencil and do his work. However, it's the teacher's job to "make" him pick up his pencil and work. The Stoplight is a crystal clear analogy to use in turning around a defiant student. Your student will see the bigger picture, and should begin working on-task immediately. You can use The Stoplight in the classroom or one-on-one with a student. I often employ the Stoplight technique with the student in front of his parents and his counselor. When using the Stoplight in front of other adults, you can expect a positive reaction from the adults in the room and a look of resignation from the defiant student, who knows he's busted.

Here is how it works. I'll play the teacher, and, Bill, you be the recalcitrant student.

BILL:
Okay.

TOM:
Bill, have you ever been in a car with your Mom?

BILL:
Yeah.

TOM:
And when you're in the car with your Mom and the traffic light turns red, what does she do?

BILL:
She stops.

TOM:
And let's say the light turns green, Bill. What does she do next?

BILL:
Well, she hits the gas and goes.

TOM:
Okay, great, Bill. That's right. The job of the light is to give your Mom her directions. And your Mom's job is to what?

BILL:
Follow them.

TOM:
And let me ask you something else. If your Mom yells at the stoplight, is it going to change any quicker?

BILL:
No, of course not.

TOM:
Is it personal? Is the traffic light mad at your Mom, and that's why it turned red?

BILL:

Well, no.

TOM:

Right. It's just the way it is. The job of the traffic light is to simply give your Mom directions. And your Mom's job is to follow them. Bill, as your teacher, my job is exactly like that stop light. It is nothing personal. My job is to give you directions, and your job is to, what?

BILL:

Ignore them, you stupid teacher!

TOM:

Actually, you might get that response! In fact, you can almost count on some angry sarcasm. In that case, I might say, "That's not an

☀ *Chalk Talk*

The red light/green light illustration was very helpful in several conferences I held with students and their parents. It eliminates the "blame game" of some parents who think the teacher is at fault when their child doesn't follow directions and do their work. ADHD children often work well one-on-one at home but have difficulty in large group settings like the classroom. Parents often think the personality of the teacher is the problem.

Carolyn D., New York, New York

I discussed with one boy how sometimes it feels as though everyone is against you when you hit every red light. Life isn't always fair but you have to follow the laws and the rules. After that we discussed different scenarios in the classroom and related it to the story. Things seemed much more clear to him!!

Sarah Z., Philadelphia, Pennsylvania

appropriate answer. Come on now, you know the answer we are looking for." Then I just wait patiently as an uncomfortable silence fills the room. Every adult in the room will instantly recognize how reasonable you're being, and how you're calmly explaining your role as a professional educator. This is an incredible tool that makes a lasting impact on that student. That's because when you use The Stoplight you're being reasonable, and students intuitively understand that this is how the teacher-student process works.

BILL:
I would also think that this analogy is helpful for the rest of the class to hear — if you're doing this in the classroom — because it not only provides your students a good context in which to view your future directions but also may put the class on your side in this particular dispute.

TOM:
The beauty of it is that it's not confrontational, but it is *direct*. When a student tells you, "You can't tell me what to do," utilizing The Stoplight clearly shows them that it *is* the job of a teacher to give them directions, and that their job is to follow them. And that it's nothing personal.

BILL:
How long have you been using The Stoplight?

TOM:
I think about 12 years now. I was introduced to the idea in a school district seminar, and the idea stuck with me. I was introduced to the idea in a school district seminar. Although I'm not sure, the speaker may have been Randy Sprick, which wouldn't surprise me because he has many wonderful ideas on education.

Points to remember from Chapter 11

▶ The Stoplight is a tool makes an impact and rarely backfires.

▶ Use the Stoplight for students who won't follow directions quickly and quietly the first time given.

▶ When you use The Stoplight, students intuitively understand that this is how the teacher-student process is supposed to work.

▶ When used in front of adults, The Stoplight will make you appear reasonable, professional, and increases your credibility.

▶ The Stoplight is only one technique to use with oppositional students. Please read the Chapter 6 on "Right Words" for additional strategies.

Teacher Quick Write #14

Using your own words, practice The Stoplight by writing it out. Then practice saying it one time by using a friend or colleague in a role-play.

CHAPTER 12

How to give directions in your classroom that students will follow quickly and quietly

TOM:

I have five guidelines that will help teachers to convince children with ADHD to follow directions quickly and quietly. Here they are:

1. **Only give directions that are specific and crystal clear. You'll increase compliance and avoid power struggles.**

    For example, don't say to an ADHD kid, "You need to enter the room nicely." That phrase is not clear. You need to use seeable, doable language. Instead say, "Enter the room with your hands at your side." That example comes from Dolores Cook's, "Positive Approaches to Teaching." In another one of her examples, she tells ADHD students, "Do you know what *listen* means? *Listen* means that your mouth is closed, and that your eyes are on my mouth." That's what I mean by being crystal clear and using seeable, doable language.

2. **Never argue with or nag your ADHD students.**

As the saying goes, arguing with a troubled kid is like mud wrestling a pig — you both get muddy, and the pig enjoys it. Arguing will not work. It's counter-productive.

3. **Keep accurate records about all problems and confrontations. Write down everything a disruptive child says and does, using exact quotes and as much specific information as you can.**

   Quote him, and have a clipboard handy where you can quickly write this type of information down. It's a good idea to create a special notebook for this purpose. For example, if a student is talking in class or giving me some sort of difficulty, as soon as I get the chance I will open up my notebook to the page that has that student's file. On that page I'll write, *I asked Andy to do his math. His book was open to the right page, and I told him, "You need to get started on the assignment." But Andy put his head down and he refused to do the work. I came back to his desk three minutes later and I said, "Andy, it looks like you're refusing to get started on your work." Then he said to me, "I don't have to do this stuff, it's boring."* See how I document everything he said with direct quotes? That's what you want to do (inconspicuously, of course).

You document everything on paper. Then, Andy later finds out that you've called his mother and gave her a word-by-word accounting of the situation, he not only becomes more accountable but now you are not in a position in which it becomes his word against yours. Why? Because you only reported the facts and you used his own words as evidence against himself! No one, including the parent, can accuse you of personal bias because you didn't call the mother to say something like, "Well, Andy's a bad kid." **No, instead, you simply recited a transcript of exactly what happened.** That puts you in a better position.

Here's the trick for making this work perfectly: **Don't lose your cool**. Continue to be calm, even if the student becomes inappropriate and aggravating. You need to be like a court reporter in your detachment. Simply know that you're going to document all this,

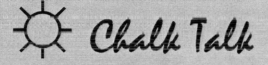

Chalk Talk

I found that keeping a record of the frequency, type and strength of the misbehavior of particular students in a way that was evident to the students themselves was in itself a good deterrent to those and other students. My pen and clipboard became the equivalent of a security camera.

Mary C., Australia

which will put you in a great position for the next parent-teacher conference or other meeting. Now you have a transcript of how *reasonable* you were. I cannot emphasize the importance of this enough. This will make you look credible and fair to the parent, and the principal will be impressed if the matter ever gets to her desk.

BILL:
So no matter how inappropriate this student becomes, you remain calm.

TOM:
Yes. The more unreasonable he is, the more reasonable you want to remain. You know in the back of your mind that you're going to write this down on your next break. That will give you immediate peace in that moment, which will count for a *lot*!

When you keep your cool, you'll benefit from a feeling of being more in control. I recommend creating a clipboard or a chart to document the frequency, duration and force of student behaviors. In other words, how often does the behavior occur, how long is each negative episode, and how intense is the behavior? Use the Student Misbehavior Records/Forms found in my bonus materials.

Now, let's say a kid is getting out of his seat during instruction and it's become an ongoing battle. You use the student misbehavior chart and make a hash mark each time he gets out of his seat. It will take you the briefest of moments to make a hash mark on your pre-prepared chart. And when you do that for several days in a row, you now have the proper ammunition to talk about the problem. You'll be able to say, "You know, every day I've been keeping track of Andy getting out of his seat during class. And over a half-hour period each day, he's getting out of his seat eight times. And I've tried these strategies and he's still doing it four times. So can we come up with some other ideas on how to solve this problem?" And then the group can brainstorm ideas on how to improve the situation.

BILL:
What if these ideas don't succeed in changing the student's behavior?

TOM:
Then go back to the drawing board and try even more interventions.

> *When you keep your cool, you'll benefit from a feeling of being more in control.*

BILL:
Okay, so you try intervention after intervention and you document your efforts. What if things still don't improve?

TOM:
If that's the case, then perhaps the school district employs a behavior specialist who can bring a fresh set of eyes to the situation. Or, maybe the school administration should consider looking at whether this child is placed in the right classroom. He might need a more restrictive placement where he can be successful. He may need a shortened school day or some one-on-one help. But if you barge into the administrator's office and say, "Andy doesn't belong in my class because he's always out of his seat!" and you have no documentation, you'll look like an unreasonable and ineffective teacher who can't handle her class. As far as the assistant principal knows, "always out of his seat" means only twice a week. That's why written documentation will make you look terrific — and can ultimately lead to solving Andy's specific problem.

146

4. "No" must always mean "no."

When you give directions, never be wishy-washy. If you say you're going to do X, then follow through and do X. For example, let's say you've given a class assignment and one of your students, Wendy, refuses to begin work. So you walk next to her desk and calmly whisper in a matter-of-fact tone, "Wendy, you need to start doing your work. If you choose to start doing your work, you'll get credit like everyone else. But if you don't start working, then I'm going to have to call your mom. **It's your choice,** either way." Then you walk next to her desk three minutes later and calmly whisper, "Wendy, it looks like you've chosen to not start your work, so I'm going to call your mom." *And then you follow through and call her mother.* As I mentioned already, I sometimes do it right there from the classroom. I say to the parent, "Wendy's having a hard time getting started on her math — can you talk with her?" Then I hand the phone to Wendy and say, "Wendy, your mom wants to talk to you." That kind of phone call often results with the child apologizing for his actions and the rest of the class re-focusing on their work to avoid the same consequence.

5. Control your emotions.

Always state negative consequences in a clear and matter-of-fact tone. Save your emotion for your praise statements, because your ADHD kids are seeking emotional responses from you.

> **Don't yell at your kids. If you reserve your emotion for your praise statements, you'll improve your class management.**

BILL:
So that means not raising your voice and yelling at a kid?

TOM:

Right. You're letting the kids win when you submit to that impulse. However, when I spot a kid trying hard, then I'll react with some real positive emotion. You'll see the excitement in my face. This shows kids that the only way to get an emotional reaction from the teacher is by making a meaningful contribution.

BILL:

I'd like to bring up a point that maybe you'll take issue with . . . Isn't it true that if you show too much emotion in praising a kid for something that's not that big of a deal, that you come off sounding insincere? I hear about so many positive reinforcement awards designed to build self-esteem that I can't help but feel that their effect is lost on kids. I think kids can see through that.

TOM:

Excellent point. You know, Dale Carnegie wrote about the difference between praise and flattery. He said that mere flattery comes off insincere and is spoken in general terms. For instance, telling a kid "Oh, great job!" for a task they've already mastered will come off sounding cheap. On the other hand, true praise is specific and accompanied by emotion and a smile.

Some kids react negatively to praise, so announcing your praise to those students in front of everyone else will not feel like a reward to them. In that case, it is better to say something to him privately, or in passing. You could catch him quickly as he is leaving your classroom, or maybe you could say something to him during a Walk and Talk, but the bottom line is if you individualize or customize your praise it will hit the mark.

> *Tell the student exactly what you liked about what he accomplished, instead of some general praise statement that sounds generic.*

Tell the student exactly what you liked about what he accomplished, instead of some general praise statement that sounds generic. Tell the student that you liked how he mixed the colors on a certain art piece instead of just saying, "Great job." But remember to only give compliments you sincerely feel are warranted.

Here's another guideline: only reinforce and strongly compliment _emerging behaviors_.

I'll give you a ridiculous example to illustrate the point. A mother telling her two-year-old, "Good potty!" when the child successfully uses the toilet is appropriate praise. But if the child is 17 years old and has been using the bathroom efficiently for 15 years, Mom standing in the hallway and clapping, "Good potty!" is not a quality praise statement here and it also indicates a serious problem on mom's part! That's an absurd example, but it points out the timing issue of praising emerging behaviors.

If you praise a child for something he already has mastered, it gives him the feeling — and rightly so — that you don't really know him. And there's a bit of respect that can be lost when that happens.

That being said, look for creative ways to increase your sincere and specific praise statements. That is a powerful tool in turning disruptive students into your best ones.

Teacher Quick Write #15

Think of one activity you do regularly in your class in which you could increase compliance by using more specific and clear language. Write out how those clear directions might sound.

_____

_____

_____

_____

_____

Points to remember from Chapter 12

▶ Follow these five rules in giving directions:

- Only give crystal clear directions.
- Never argue or nag.
- Write down what a child does and says.
- No must always mean no.
- Control your emotions.

▶ Give specific and meaningful compliments.

▶ Customize praise statements and realize that not all kids react positively to public, over-generalized compliments.

▶ Reinforce emerging behaviors.

▶ Look for creative ways to consistently and sincerely praise your students.

CHAPTER 13

Creating responsibility in the classroom

TOM:
"Creating Responsibility in the Classroom" is an idea from Thomas Sergiovanni. Typically, many teachers go through their day catching kids on various classroom infractions. They're busting them like a traffic cop. *Don't do this, don't do that.* And what do you hear in return from the kids?

BILL:
Lots of complaints, justifications and finger pointing.

TOM:
Right. Instead of playing the role of cop, take on the role of Moses. That's what Sergiovanni advocates. Instead of saying, "You broke this rule," you point out a set of rules the classroom created together. You remind them of their own commitment *to each other*.

BILL:
How do you set this up?

TOM:
As a teacher, you establish certain class rules. One thing you can do is develop those class rules on the first day of school with the entire class and try to involve all students in the creation of their class rules. Keep the rules simple and short.

Here are five sample rules:

1. Follow directions quickly and quietly.

2. Do your best work.

3. Respect yourself and others.

4. Be on time.

5. Keep your hands and feet to yourself.

BILL:
Those rules are general. Is that what works best?

TOM:
Yes, that's ideal, but the wording needs modifications for older students. For high school students I would just eliminate rule number 5 from the above sample rules.

BILL:
Going back to the basic idea . . . forming the class rules *with* your students allows the class an opportunity to create the rules, which means you are in alliance with them and not adversarial foes. Do I have that right?

TOM:
Yes. **And so when a student violates one of the class rules, you simply remind him of a rule that he created.**

The best way to enforce the class rules is to post your rules somewhere visible in the classroom. I actually post them in the front of the room and the back of the room. I write them in large letters in the front of the room, so that everyone can see them. For example, for rule number one I simply write, "Follow directions." **I also post the rules in the back of the room in large letters, so that I am reminded to use them in my praise statements.** This works especially well with younger students. For instance, if I see that Angela is starting her work right away, I can say, "Good job on following directions quickly and quietly, Angela" . . . or I might say, "Jackie is doing a great job over here, and one of our rules is doing your best work, so way to go, Jackie." **So I use the rules in my praise statements; that's crucial.**

BILL:
How does an acting-out student develop that sort of accountability?

TOM:
It's all about students accepting responsibility for their actions. When something "bad" happens that student invariably says, "It wasn't me," or "I didn't do it." Can you imagine the problems he will have in life if he constantly thinks and says those statements? He obviously needs to accept responsibility for the part that *was* his fault. He needs to say, "This is what I did wrong," and, "This is what I should have done differently."

Here are five steps for helping students realize where they stepped

Chalk Talk

An idea from your book that has already helped me is the Student Responsibility Form. Here is what happened: On the very first day of school a student took three book covers from a classmate's desk and said that they belonged to him. The owner of the book covers reported the incident to me. At first I did not know whom to believe. Since it was time for our math class, I did not have time at that moment to discuss the issue with the students. So I quickly modified the Student Responsibility Form. I added: "Describe the book covers. Tell me something special about the book covers that will help me to know that they belong to you." I gave a form to each student to complete and continued with my math lesson. During our independent reading period I read what both students had written and examined the book covers. The book covers actually belonged to the girl because she wrote that she had used her marker to color the kitten's eyes purple. We all could see that the kitten's eyes had been colored purple. Using that form solved the problem without disrupting the class.

Janice Hixon, third grade, Columbus, Georgia

153

out of line and exactly how they upset the classroom community. You can turn this list into a poster or copy it onto individual sheets of paper so that the student who's in trouble can read and answer the questions in private. I have included these five steps in The ADHD Solution Workbook.

Ask the student appropriate questions in the following sequence:

> 1. (The Events.) *What happened? What did I do wrong?*

> 2. (Social Contract.) *What are our agreements to each other?*

> 3. (Moral Connection.) *Why is what happened wrong?*

> 4. (Next Steps.) *How will this be fixed? (Note: one of the "next steps" here should be an appropriate consequence linked to the student's misdeed).*

> 5. (Revisit Commitment.) *What is our commitment to each other?*

BILL:
Let's take this through a specific example.

TOM:
Okay. Let's say Mike pushed Susie on the playground. You sit him down and ask:

- *What happened? What did I do wrong?* "Susie was in front of me and I wanted to use the slide, and it was my turn. I pushed Susie."

- *What are our agreements to each other?* "Keep our hands and feet to ourselves and respect others."

- *Why is what happened wrong?* "Well, I guess Susie could have gotten hurt or fallen."

154

- *How will this be fixed?* "I'll tell Susie I'm sorry her pants ripped and I will talk to my Dad about giving Susie's parents money to buy new pants."

- *What is our commitment to each other?* "We don't allow any pushing in our school, and I won't push Susie or anyone else again."

BILL:
So, basically, using this list will address a problem situation and may prevent it from recurring.

TOM:
Yes, because you're not coming down on Mike by saying, "You did this wrong and here is the punishment." It encourages him to reflect on what he did, and then it guides him into doing things differently next time. However, you must also assign him an additional consequence for pushing Susie. You can even take this a step further by using this as a role-playing exercise in class.

BILL:
How would that work?

TOM:
Well, if you hang these five steps as a poster, you could spend time in the classroom talking about "Creating Community in the Classroom." It's effective that way. You just create various scenarios where someone has done something wrong and you role-play with different students on answering the questions.

Another way to do this is to simplify the whole "Creating Community in the Classroom" concept by handing a student the Student Responsibility Form they do something wrong. And on that form are the five reflective questions we mentioned. Alternatively, you can use these three questions:

1. **What did I do wrong?**

2. **What should have I done differently?**

3. What will I choose to do next time?

BILL:
What do you prefer, speaking to the student or asking him to reflect on his actions in writing?

TOM:
It's best to do both. When an incident occurs you can hand-signal for a student to fill out a Student Responsibility Form in a study carrel in the back of the room. Have the forms available for this purpose. Then, when you get a natural break in your teaching routine, you can sit down with the student and go over his form. I also recommend that the teacher and student sign the form.

If another student was "wronged" by the incident, I would bring her over and have all three of us discuss the reflection form. I would also have her sign it.

BILL:
What else is important about this written self-reflection?

TOM:
It is good protection in case Susie's parent says, "Mike pushed my daughter down and you didn't do anything about it." Believe me, that conversation may indeed happen — and happen quickly. With cell phones today, Susie could come stomping in from recess, hand you her cell phone, saying, "My mom wants to talk to you *now*!"

BILL:
What would you tell Susie's mom, in this case?

TOM:
"Mrs. Martinez, I am aware of the incident. I'm teaching right now in front of the class. I can discuss this with you after math class. Does that sound okay?" Then, when I had a break I would call Mrs. Martinez and report, "Mike was in the back of the room filling out a Student Responsibility Form when you called, which is our first step in the process. After Mike completed the form, Susie, Mike and I sat down to discuss how this will be fixed. Mrs. Martinez, do you

156

remember that this was the procedure we discussed at open house? Anyway, we all sat down and talked and this is what we all agreed to…"

BILL:
Is the rest of the class listening to all this?

TOM:
Well, if this is a clear-cut case of right and wrong *and* the incident doesn't involve sexual harassment, I sometimes *intentionally* stand in front of the class so everyone can hear me speaking to Mrs. Martinez! And I would point to each step of the poster as I went along. That makes the class commitments really come alive!

Points to remember from Chapter 13

▶ Instead of playing the role of cop, take on the role of Moses and remind your students of their own commitments to each other.

▶ Set up and post your class rules and post them in the front and back of the class.

▶ Here is a list of sample rules to use or modify for your class:

- Follow directions.
- Do your best.
- Respect others.

- Be on time.
- Keep your hands to yourself.

▶ Refer to the rules in the back of the room and use them in your praise statements. Example: "Good job of following directions, Jackie."

▶ Use the following five questions to help students accept responsibility:

- What happened? What did I do wrong?
- What are our agreements?
- Why is what happened wrong?
- How will this be fixed? (Include a consequence for the misdeed).
- What is our commitment to each other?

▶ Use one of the Student Responsibility Forms, which are based on these commitments. Have students fill one out when they violate one of the community rules.

▶ Three simple questions a teacher might ask a child after an incident are:

- What did you do wrong?
- What should you have done differently?
- What will you choose to do next time?

CHAPTER 14

Conflict avoidance techniques

BILL:

How can we teach ADHD children to look before they leap? To actually think about what they're doing before they do it?

TOM:

Often, kids act impulsively, reacting upon the first idea suggested to them by someone else, or whatever pops into their creative heads. So we need conflict avoidance techniques to guide them into making better decisions and staying out of trouble.

What is the most common mistake teachers make in this regard? Well, let's try this exercise. If I repeatedly told you, "Don't think about Frankenstein, don't think about Frankenstein, don't think about Frankenstein," what do you suppose would happen?

BILL:

I would think about Frankenstein.

TOM:

Right. Instead of telling your students, "Just say NO" or, "Don't listen to those other kids, don't do that," you need to arm them with new skills that will replace those tempting behaviors with positive actions. "Just say no" isn't enough. You need to show them other strategies that will keep them safe and out of trouble.

I have a five-step problem-solving model, and once you teach these five steps, your students will do the right thing and avoid problems.

BILL:
Okay, so this is something they run through their minds before making a decision that could lead them into conflict or trouble?

TOM:
Yes. Let me outline the five steps and it will make better sense. Teach these to your class and do some role-playing with your students so that they really grasp it.

Let me list the five steps to staying out of trouble. Then, let's review each one in detail.

> *Teaching your students to "Just say no" isn't enough. You need to show them other strategies that will keep them out of trouble.*

Here are the five steps:

1. Listen and ask questions.

2. Identify the problem.

3. State the consequences that may occur.

4. Offer an alternative.

5. Leave.

BILL:
How could someone use this in a specific situation?

TOM:
Later in this chapter, I list four possible role-play scenarios you can present to your class. For now, here is an example of a role-play scenario you can present in class. The subject of this example is admittedly extreme, as it involves the subject of stealing cars, but I've used it in class and it always works great as a role-play for

students grade 7 or higher. And let's face it, some students do in fact steal and think it's okay.

Use this example for children in fifth grade and up.

Let's say your student Brian has gotten into trouble in the past for stealing things or shoplifting with his friends. His friends' names are Mike and Randy. So let's say Mike and Randy approach Brian and say, "Hey, let's go to the mall."

Step No. 1. Listen and ask questions

Now, in Step No. 1, Brian is going to **listen and ask questions**. Brian might think or say, "What exactly are we going to do at the mall?" And his friends might say, "Oh, catch a movie," or, "Just hang out". And now Brian might continue listening and asking questions. He might say, "Well, do you guys have any money for the movie?" Brian will pick up important information about what he's about to get involved with if he **keeps** asking questions. Here's how that conversation might go:

Brian: *You guys don't have any money? How are we going to get into the movie?*

Mike and Randy: *Well, movies are stupid anyway. We don't need to see a movie.*

Brian: *Okay, then what do you want to do at the mall?*

Mike and Randy: *We're going to check out a Mustang there.*

Brian: *Oh really?*

Mike and Randy: *Yeah, we're going to drive around in this Mustang.*

Brian: *Oh, Randy, is that your older brother's car? I know he has a good job and all. Is it his car we're checking out?*

Mike and Randy: *No. It's just a Mustang. And we know the keys are in it.*

So, as we can see, by listening and asking questions, it's clear that Brian's friends are going to the mall with no intention of seeing a movie or hanging out. They want to take Brian to the mall to steal a car.

BILL:
Isn't it just common sense to know what you're getting into?

TOM:
Yes, it's common sense to me and you, but for many kids who act on impulse, this is a valuable lesson to teach them.

BILL:
So now the kid has a much better understanding of the situation.

Step No. 2. Identify the problem

TOM:
Yes, and that brings us to Step No. 2, **identify the problem.** This is where the student says, **"You want me to _____?"**

BILL:
And in this case, Brian would say to Mike and Randy, "You want me to go to the mall and hop in a car that's not ours that has keys in it?"

TOM:
Yes. And, depending on the situation, Brian might not ask the question out loud. He might have grown up with Mike and Randy and knows full well what these guys are up to. So he might just process all this in his mind, which is perfectly fine, too. The key is that he identifies the problem clearly.. Each situation is different. Whether he says it out loud or keeps it to himself is his call.

Step No. 3. Recognize the consequence

And now we have the third step: **Recognize the consequence. "If I do that, _____ could happen."** And, again, he could either think this internally or discuss it out loud, depending on the situation. And now Brian, following these steps, would now be thinking,

162

"Hmm, Mike and Randy want me to go to the mall to possibly steal a car, and if I do that I could land in juvenile hall, which is something I do NOT want to do."

BILL:
And it looks as if Brian's next step is to . . .

Step No. 4. Offer an alternative

TOM:
Offer an alternative. That's what he does in Step No. 4. This is where you empower your student to redirect the situation. This is where Brian says, **"Instead of that, let's do _____."**
This step is more often said out loud and it's offered as a group alternative. In Brian's case, he might say, "Hey guys, instead of going to the mall, let's go play X-Box at my house." So the alternative activity is something that's still within the scope of what those friends like to do, but obviously is a more positive activity. It is more appropriate, but also fun.

BILL:
Looks like Step 5 is used as a last-case resort?

Step No. 5. Leave

TOM:
Yes. Step 5 is: **If needed, leave.** And I would add: Leave quickly, and leave friendly, if possible. Mike and Randy are his friends, and Brian doesn't need to turn this into a confrontation. If Brian has offered an alternative along the lines of, "Hey, instead of going to the mall, let's go to my house and watch a movie, and maybe my mom will order us a pizza," and Mike and Randy are still intent on going to the mall, then Brian simply needs to leave quickly and get himself out of this situation. The Bottom line is that Brian needs to do what is safe and smart for him. And leaving *quickly* is important, because if Brian sticks around, Mike and Randy will end up talking Brian into going with them to the mall!

BILL:
I understand you have a sixth step to all this?

163

Step No. 6. No-and-go

TOM:
Yes, the sixth step is an important one. It's to be used in case this is a dangerous situation. If the situation is dangerous, then it's just **"no-and-go."** You don't even go through the other five steps. It's a simple no-and-go.

Here's an example. Let's say a stranger pulls up in a car, rolls down the window, and asks your student if he wants to try some cocaine. You don't want this kid going through the five steps and engaging this character in a conversation and offering alternatives. You just want him out of there in a New York minute! And his parent would want him out of there, too, obviously. So that's why teaching this sixth step is so important.

In this specific case, I would teach him to firmly say no, walk in the opposite direction the car is traveling, and find a trusted adult. If the child has a cell phone, he might also dial 911. If the child is near a store, he can duck inside and call home from there.

BILL:
These steps sound great, but do they work in real life?

TOM:
Yes, they really do work, and I can't stress enough the importance of role playing these steps with your students in front of the entire class. Role play, role play, role play! Role-play these steps repeatedly, and only then will the students be able to respond in these situations automatically. Go through lots of examples with your students.

It can be a lot of fun. Take a couple students out in the hallway to set up a sample scenario/situation in which they try to convince a third student to do something, and instruct the third student use the five steps in front of the class to extricate himself from the situation.

For instance, you tell the two students that their role-playing assignment is to convince the third student to join them in ditching class. You tell these two students privately, "Okay, I want you guys to convince Joey to ditch class with you, but I don't want you to tell him you're planning on ditching, make up something." And then you pull Joey aside and tell him, "These guys will tell you that they want you to do something, but they might be up to no good. So I want you to ask lots of questions and go through the five steps we've gone over in class." And then you let it play itself out in front of the class, while you guide the interaction.

I also want to point out that the car-stealing situation is just an outrageous example to start the role plays rolling. You have other issues that are more pertinent to your class, including school-related issues. I recommend role-playing those types of things.

> *I can't stress enough the importance of role-playing these steps with your students in front of the entire class. Role-play these steps repeatedly, and only then will the students be able to respond in these situations automatically.*

BILL:
Will teachers have time to teach these "off-subject" skills? I know that everyone is concerned about test scores and "the basics," so what do you have to say about that? How important is working these things into teachers' lesson plans . . . and how practical is it?

TOM:
Teaching the basics are obviously the No. 1 responsibility of our schools today, no question about it. That's our job. But it's also true that kids need to be taught how to "do school," stay out of trouble, and avoid succumbing to peer pressure. Teaching kids effective decision-making skills will set the table for success at any level.

I would suggest teaching these skills in the first week of class. And I'd use the last five minutes of the hour to role play these throughout the year.

BILL:
What about the issue of teaching morality? I know that many people are concerned that teaching these sorts of techniques borders on controversial "morality instruction."

TOM:
Every teacher is already teaching some set of morality; it's just a matter of whether they're teaching it explicitly or implicitly. **Kids need to be taught how to treat each other with respect and kindness, and how to make good decisions.** Our society is becoming much more fragmented now, without the family and social supports we've had in decades past, and that's why teachers take on these large, valuable roles.

I think teachers need to focus on teaching. However, when you role play specific strategies that encourage students to think through their problems, they become better students and better people.

BILL:
What about logistically? Do teachers have time to teach this material?

TOM:
Yes, it's too important *not* to, because it will save you time later on when students are using these techniques to stay on-task and completing assignments, rather than disrupting your class and putting you in a situation where you're continually putting out fires and going home feeling stressed and overwhelmed. Every smart teacher during her first week of class spends a lot of time reviewing the rules, and that's a good time to implement these materials.

Be proactive and you won't need to send kids to the office — that will make a good impression on your supervisors. In addition, school-wide suspensions will be reduced, which will impress your district and the state department of education.

> *I would suggest teaching these skills in the first week of class. And I'd use the last five minutes of the hour to role-play these throughout the year.*

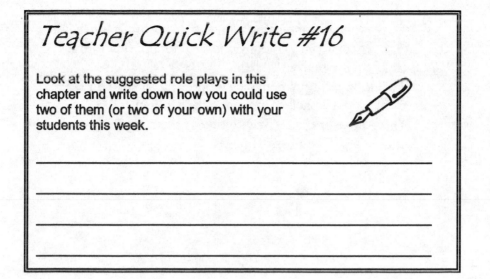

Teacher Quick Write #16

Look at the suggested role plays in this chapter and write down how you could use two of them (or two of your own) with your students this week.

_____

_____

_____

_____

Points to remember from Chapter 14

▶ Post and role-play these six steps to avoid problems:

- Listen and ask questions.
- Identify the problem.
- State the possible consequences.
- Offer an alternative.
- Leave.
- When in danger, Say "No!" and then go.

▶ Ideas for role-play might include:

- Two students convincing a third student to lie for them.
- One student trying to convince another student to put tacks on the teacher's chair.
- Two kids trying to convince a third kid to steal an MP3 from the backpack of an unpopular student.
- Three boys at the mall, with two of them walking behind a girl and harassing her.

 CHAPTER 15

Six strategies to silence chatterboxes

TOM:
Nothing can bring a productive classroom to a grinding halt faster than an incessant "chatterbox." Unfortunately, our first inclinations in quieting a chatterbox will backfire and worsen the problem.

BILL:
What should a teacher *not* do when trying to quiet a chatterbox?

TOM:
First of all, don't "Shhhh" the class! When you shush the class in this manner, or say something like "Joey, you need to stop talking," you are actually reinforcing the behavior. You are strengthening the probability the students will continue to chatter away. In other words, it is negative reinforcement without any real consequence. For the teacher, this amounts to self-defeating behavior.

Use these six strategies instead:

1. **Planned ignoring:** If the student is chatting during an activity, reinforce those students who are still working on-task. Shower reinforcement on those who are working well in close proximity to the chatterbox. For example, if Joey is

goofing off, walk up to his on-task seatmate and say, "Nice job of working, John!"

2. **Reinforce other students for ignoring chatters.** Offer some sort of reward or positive consequence to anyone who ignores a nearby chatterbox. For example, if Ashley knows that by ignoring Jason she will get five extra minutes of lunch, she will be more likely to resist the urge to attend to his acting-out behavior. Teaching students to ignore a chatty student is an important emerging behavior to reinforce.

3. **Use proximity to your advantage:** Move around and watch how your positioning in the classroom will silence the chatterbox. Consider pulling up a chair and quietly performing the same activity nearby. This is a great strategy that often works wonders!

> *Move around and watch how your positioning in the classroom will silence the chatterbox.*

4. **Catch 'em being good:** Whenever the chatterbox is working on-task, comment, praise and reward him. It's important to reward new behaviors as soon as they are shown! The quicker you can reinforce a newly displayed behavior, the better.

5. **Utilize the "Time Owed" Concept.** If your class is held just before recess, lunch, or the end of the day, make a private note to penalize time-wasters in the following manner: At the end of class, circulate throughout the room and inform each student who "owes time." Use a time amount between two and five minutes. Say something like, "Jason, please stay seated, you owe me three minutes." Then ignore him as he sits there. Do not interact with him during the time owed! You could put an egg timer on the teacher's desk, or simply make note of the clock. Note: two to five minutes is an effective length for this technique, regardless of the student's age.

6. **Make use of charting and reinforcing:** Keep a colored chart on the wall which tracks the number of students who did not "owe time" each day. Like the traditional

fundraising thermometer chart, students see how good behavior adds up. Each time "the thermometer" becomes full, offer a class reward. This will exert peer pressure on kids to stop goofing off. Also consider individual rewards for students who reach a predetermined number of days without owing time.

Chalk Talk

I had a student in class who was constantly pushing the buttons of the other students. After reading this book, I realized this was how he was getting attention. I worked with the "targeted" students, helping them ignore the button-pusher and to stay with the lesson. Within a few days, the button-pusher realized he was not getting the response he wanted and his targets were not getting so upset. His taunting began to decrease. I'm looking forward to the results we'll get by using some of these strategies right from day one of the new school year!

Carol N., Mansfield, Texas

I had a student misbehaving. He would not yield answers, not remain in his seat, and act aggressively. He had a hard time getting along and did not know how to make friends. I read some sections in your book that outlined things that I was not supposed to do but that I *was* doing. For example, I was calling his name constantly and responding negatively to his negative behavior. But when I started to say his name to reinforce positive behavior instead of the negative ones, it made a difference for both of us.

Sonia S., Greensboro, North Carolina

BILL:
Are there any other ideas teachers should consider?

TOM:
Yes. Ask yourself these questions:

- **Are your materials part of the problem?** Increased chattering in class could be due to your teaching materials.

- **Is the work too easy or too hard?**

- **Does the chattering student have the proper materials?**

- **Are you boring them?** Take an objective look at how the work is presented. Or better yet, videotape your class and ask a friend or trusted colleague to watch the tape to solicit his or her opinion. Visit the classrooms of outstanding teachers and pick up tips on improving your presentation.

- **Would more consistent contact with parents improve the situation?** Here's a solution to your problem: Call the home of a problem chatterer every Sunday night to say hi to the parents and discuss the situation in a light manner. In three weeks or less your classroom will be much quieter.

BILL:
Is there any way to channel the negative behavior into a positive one?

TOM:
Sometimes it's best to let the student go on his "roll" for a short time. Once he sees it's not drawing any attention from you or the class, it may stop. For chatterboxes who like to roam out of their seats, give them an errand to run that takes them out of the classroom for a short while. The student could run books back to the library, deliver papers to an office, or any other pre-planned errand.

Here's one more idea: Reinforce incompatible behaviors.
Perhaps you've seen the poster of the girl swimming underwater with the caption, "It's hard to smoke pot when you're swimming underwater." Put this philosophy to work in concrete ways. For example, while you are reading "Charlotte's Web" to the class, have your students make animal shapes out of clay. By doing this, an annoying student cannot easily tap on his desk since his hands are

172

busy with the clay. This technique is known as differential reinforcement, and is a powerful tool.

Teacher Quick Write #17

How will I use planned ignoring coupled with time owed in my class as a way to silence chatterboxes? _____

_____

_____

_____

_____

_____

#18 What are three things I will do to make my class more exciting to all my students? _____

_____

_____

_____

Points to remember from Chapter 15

▶ Never "Shhh" the class.

▶ Use these six strategies to silence a chatterbox:

1. Ignore students off-task.
2. Reward kids for ignoring a nearby chatterbox.
3. Move around the classroom frequently.
4. Reward the chatterbox when he is on-task.
5. Penalize time-wasters by keeping them after class for two to five minutes.
6. Use a class chart as a motivator to exert peer pressure on chatterboxes.

▶ Honestly assess your teaching by asking the following questions:

- Are your materials part of the problem?
- Is the work too easy or too hard?
- Does the chattering student have the proper materials?
- Are you boring them?
- Would more consistent contact with parents improve the situation?

▶ Reinforce incompatible behaviors. Example: If a child constantly taps his pencil, give him something to do with his hands.

 CHAPTER 16

Eight secrets that eliminate ADHD behaviors in the classroom

TOM:
Here are some highly effective ways to reduce or eliminate problematic behaviors that teachers often see from ADHD students:

1. Use pre-arranged hand signals.

Students must learn to monitor their own behavior. This technique teaches them to do that, and heads off disruptive behavior at the same time. Let's say a student has a problem staying in his seat. What you can do is arrange a hand signal with him. If he starts to feel restless, maybe he raises two fingers to get up for half a minute to walk around. Then you acknowledge his hand signal with an affirmative nod. He goes outside for some fresh air. The student must stay within your view through the door or window. He knows he is allowed this small break because you've made this arrangement with him beforehand.

Another scenario might be that the student holds up four fingers, and by prearranged agreement the teacher knows that the student has a scheduled errand. For example, the student could take the attendance sheet to the office and then return. That would be an example of a pre-arranged hand signal along with pre-arranged errand. The entire thing is non-verbal. Neither you nor the student has to say anything. This means no classroom disruptions!

BILL:
Could it also work the other way around? Could the teacher give a prearranged signal to the student?

TOM:
Yes, those are effective, too. For example, you may have a hand signal that means "Stop." And maybe this signal means that the student must put his head down on the desk for 30 seconds as a cooling off period. That one would be for younger students, obviously, but you get the idea. Or maybe the stop signal means that the student is to take his work and go to the study carrel in the back of the room, where there will be fewer distractions.

BILL:
Okay, the two-finger signal to take a break to go outside the classroom — wouldn't that just invite trouble with students taking advantage of the arrangement to just skate out of class for a while?

TOM:
Well, obviously, you have to monitor if it's being overused. You don't want to be manipulated. If you feel it's being abused, then you need to limit his breaks or come up with something else. But remember that an ADHD student is different from other kids his age — he may not have the same control over his restlessness. His ability to sit still and "do school" (without frequent breaks) is far below that of his school loving seatmates. Pre-arranged hand signals is an effective technique aimed with that student in mind.

Look at it this way: Would you prefer this student blurting out and taking everyone off-task, or would you rather have him learn to self monitor his behavior and slip out the door with a minimum of disruption? He's going to disrupt your class one way or the other —

you might as well pick the path of least disruption ahead of time. This is a technique that smoothly accomplishes that.

2. Chunk up tasks.

Don't hand ADHD students huge, long assignments to complete all at once. Chunk them up into smaller groups of questions or tasks. You can do this for everyone, not just your ADHD kids. Let's say you're about to give a difficult exam. Instead of giving it all in one day with 100 questions, why not break it up over four days by giving them 25 questions per day.

Breaking up larger tasks into smaller, more manageable chunks will reduce the frustration level of your ADHD students. Try to avoid overwhelming your ADHD students.

3. Use student-to-student compliments.

Get students accustomed to complimenting each other. At the end of each day, say, "Okay, guys, you need to say a compliment about someone else in the class, and it can't be about what they're wearing, and it can't be what they look like." This usually ends up being about what someone else did that day. For example, "I like the way you painted the background in that picture." And when the recipient of the compliment hears it, he is to simply say, "Thank you," and then you can move onto the next student. I even had my system set up where I had a chart with compliment boxes on it to keep track. And this sheet went home with the students. This is how you get students thinking and talking positively.

> *Get students accustomed to complimenting each other. Student-to-student compliments make kids feel closer to each other and help build a friendly classroom environment.*

Some students will receive more compliments than others. As the teacher, be aware of this problem and find ways to encourage students to complement those "less popular" students. Or, find a way to make your own anonymous teacher compliments.

177

BILL:
That seems like an idea for elementary school. Can you adapt this compliment tracking system for high school kids?

TOM:
Sure. Here's one way: While students make oral presentations, everyone listening must jot down three things they really liked about the presentation, with only one corrective (or negative) statement. Student-to-student compliments make kids feel closer to each other and they help build a friendly classroom environment.

4. Use teacher-to-student compliments.

If you increase the number of times you compliment your students, you'll decrease the amount of negative classroom behavior. Students are looking for your emotional reactions. So, reserve those emotions for your praise statements!

I've heard it said before that for every negative phrase you say to your students, you should say three to four positive comments. You're looking for a good ratio of positive and encouraging comments to negative comments. Think about it — if you looked at everything you've said to an ADHD student, day in and day out, your ratio is more likely something like 10 negative for every positive. So look for ways to turn that around.

5. Use community-based instruction.

Community Based Instruction (CBI) simply means getting out of the classroom, taking your students to appropriate places that will supplement your classroom instruction.

BILL:
What if some teachers cannot take their students off-campus?

TOM:
You can get much of the same benefit by just walking around campus with your students: creating videos, doing science experiments, or walking somewhere adjacent to the campus. Or you could get parental and administrative approval to go on a field trip.

BILL:

Why is taking your kids out of the classroom a good thing?

TOM:

ADHD children often thrive outside the classroom but are terrible inside the classroom. That's just the way it is with ADHD kids. They can't stand it in the classroom and will often underperform. This is a strategy that plays toward their strengths.

BILL:

What are the logistical hurdles in getting permission for field trips?

TOM:

Well, they don't have to be big hurdles. Just talk to your fellow teachers and your site administrators. I took my high school kids to a junior college campus and nearby four-year university. In these brief visits, they became accustomed to being on a college campus, and some students were saying, "Hey, I'm going to go to that college." Just by walking around the college campus they were able to visualize themselves being there in the near future. Believe it or not, that kind of "prep work" is significant. For the students who were intimidated by higher education, those walks demystified the whole thing and took away that fear.

☼ *Chalk Talk*

I teach fifth grade and read aloud to my students for 15 to 20 minutes at the end of each school day. Usually, I read a Newbery Award novel. I try to vary the subject of the novel each time so that most of the students will be interested, but you cannot interest every child in every novel. I used the idea from Chapter 16 of asking a question after every three to five sentences to keep each student engaged. It really changed the attention paid to the book. I also used the technique of putting students' names at the ends of the questions throughout the day in all classes. Anything to keep the students interested!

Luanne D., Drexel, North Carolina

6. When speaking or reading to the class, only read or speak three to five sentences and then ask a question.

If you read more than three to five sentences from a book before asking a question, you very likely have lost the attention of your ADHD children.

Here's a good story. Once, as my father was about to address a large auditorium of teenagers, he noticed a potential agitator in the third row. So after speaking three sentences he asked the young man, "What's your opinion of what I just said?" By doing so, he hooked the kid as well as the entire audience.

Remember that reading sentences transmits information, while questions force the listener to retrieve and verify information.

BILL:
How can a teacher ask meaningful questions as she's reading to the class?

TOM:
Here's the best way: put Post-It Notes in the text with your questions written on them. Just put the notes right on the pages. And as you (or the students) read along, your questions will be right there.

> *The bottom line is, if you just talk at students, they won't retain anything. So asking frequent questions is a powerful strategy.*

The bottom line is, if you just talk *at* the students, they won't retain anything. So, asking frequent questions is a powerful strategy to use with all kids, but especially so with ADHD children. So read a few sentences and ask a question, read a few sentences and ask a question. If you're reading more than three to five sentences at a time without asking a question, you're not being effective. You're losing part of your class, and your ADHD kids will start acting up.

Here's another trick: Don't just call on the students who volunteer answers. Pick someone else. And when you do call on a student, put his name at the *end* of the question.

180

For instance, as you're reading along you ask, "Who is a good friend of Eric the Lionhearted . . . *Ronnie?*" You see, when I put Ronnie's name at the end, it makes everyone listens to the entire question.

If you use the student's name at the beginning of the question, you're only requiring that one student listen. Try it both ways to see what I mean:

- "Is Ivanhoe a good friend of Eric the Lionhearted . . . What do you think, *Ronnie?*"

- "*Ronnie!* Is Ivanhoe a good friend of Eric the Lionhearted?*"

In the first example, no one knows to whom you're going to direct this question. In the second example, everyone knows right off the bat that only Ronnie is on the hook and their minds can easily wander.

However, try your own variation of these techniques. Keep in mind the purpose of frequent questioning is to keep the class engaged and vested in the discussion not to punish students who have severe distractibility.

Here's another key in teaching ADHD kids. **When teaching vocabulary, only teach three to five words per day.** Now this may seem ridiculous to us old-time teachers. But if you limit your vocabulary list to three to five new words, and you spend time on each of those words — explaining what they mean, using them in various contexts, looking them up in the dictionary, and writing sentences using those words — then those kids are going to leave your class that day remembering and using those three to five words. They'll retain them much better.

If you throw them a vocabulary list of 20 new words, your ADHD kids aren't going to remember any of them. Five new words four times a week still adds up to 20 new words per week. That's significant. And, more importantly, you made sure that your students internalized the information because you chunked it up over a few different sessions.

7. Give your students some choice in determining their work.

If you lay out a few choices, they're going to feel empowered and excited about completing the assignment they select. And the thing is, you can still make it the same assignment, essentially. You're just giving them a subtle choice as to the form of the work.

8. Use project-based learning as a way to teach new material.

There's evidence that project-based learning is beneficial. Just because your class is sitting quietly listening to you doesn't mean you're providing the best learning situation. For example, you can obtain games and simulations in which students are part of, say, a Native American tribe. In these game simulations, some students play the role of European settlers, while others play the role of Native Americans, and then both sides learn the material in a fresh, memorable way. That's just a quick example. But anything the kids actually *do* — will cause them to remember and learn material better than by just sitting and passively receiving it.

☼ Chalk Talk

We have implemented a system of signals (tap on shoulder for settle, thumbs up for "You've done well", "T" with hands for toilet break), as well as permanent passes (toilet pass, library pass, red card emergency to be taken to office on signal) that avoid distracting interruptions and creates an environment of mutual respect and trust. More time is spent on task as well.

Liz G., Hazelbrook, Australia

Points to remember from Chapter 16

▶ Use these eight secrets to eliminate ADHD behaviors in your classroom:

1. Use pre-arranged hand signals.
2. Chunk up big tasks into manageable parts.
3. Provide a daily, systematic forum for student-to-student compliments.
4. Praise a student far more then you criticize him.
5. Use permission slips and perform community-based instruction to get ADHD children outside.
6. Only speak (or read) three to five sentences in a row before asking a good question.
7. Give students some choice in determining their work.
8. Use projects; kids remember what they do.

Teacher Quick Write #19

Finish these two sentences:

• "A time someone brightened my day with a compliment was _____

_____

• "A time I brightened someone else's day was _____

_____

CHAPTER 17

Mnemonic Memory Devices

TOM:

Let's talk about Mnemonic *(New-**Mon**-ic)* Memory Devices, a great tool to use with ADHD children. They're great for all kids, but they're especially important for ADHD kids.

A Mnemonic Memory Device is any type of made-up saying that triggers information you want to remember. For example, when I'm teaching graduate students, I use the following Mnemonic Device: When you prepare a speech you need to think W.E.T. You need to use the right **Words**, **Emotion**, and **Timing**. See how that works?

BILL:

Sure. It's a handy acronym that ensures recall of a batch of information.

TOM:

A Mnemonic Memory Device goes into your long-term memory and triggers information that otherwise might be hard to retrieve. For example, I might ask you to list the order of events of the Civil War. Now you could study many books on the subject, and commit it to memory somehow. But you're not going to remember it long-term. But if I teach you the following saying: "Four Bulls Ate Everything Vicky Grew," and I make you repeat that a few times, and then you draw an actual picture of four bulls eating everything Vicky grew, then, believe me, you're going to remember that phrase.

BILL:
Yes, I see what you mean. So can you translate **"Four Bulls Ate Everything Vicky Grew"** into the chronological order of events of the Civil War?

TOM:
Sure. *Four:* **Fort Sumter**, the first shots in the Civil War. *Bulls:* **Bull Run**, the first major battle. *Ate:* **Antietam**, the bloodiest battle in Civil War history with 20,000 casualties. *Everything:* **The Emancipation Proclamation**, where Lincoln abolished slavery. *Vicky:* **The Battle of Vicksburg**, which controlled the Mississippi River for the North. *Grew:* **The Gettysburg Address**, four score and seven years ago.

Now, I'm someone who can't remember history, but because I know "Four Bulls Ate Everything Vicky Grew," I always instantly and accurately recall the order of events in the Civil War. I taught this to eighth-graders 14 years ago in a 40-minute session, and none of them will ever forget.

You can search for Mnemonic Memory Devices on the Internet, but you can easily make up your own or talk to your colleagues to come up with more. For example, one of my graduate students raised his hand in class and said, "Do you know how to memorize the nine planets? Start with the planet closest to the sun and say, **'My Very Easy Method Just Set Up Nine Planets,'** and of course that is an easy way to remember Mercury, Venus, Earth, Mars, Jupiter, Saturn, Uranus, Neptune, and Pluto.

Mnemonic Memory Devices are perfectly suited for geography, among other topics. I taught West Coast geography using "Cow Can Can." That means California, Oregon, Washington up the coast, California, Arizona, New Mexico to the east, and California, Arizona, Nevada up top.

Kids love these sayings, and they love to develop their own, too. When I taught the states around New Jersey, I told them, **"New**

Jersey Cows Run In Mud." That one translates to: New Jersey, Connecticut, Rhode Island, and Massachusetts.

Another commonly taught one involves the Cardinal Directions: north, east, south, west . . . or, **"Never Eat Shredded Wheat."** That's an old one that's been taught for ages.

In teaching the Great Lakes, and starting with Lake Superior on the left, you can teach, **"Super Man Helps Every One** for Lake Superior, Lake Michigan, Lake Huron, Lake Erie, Lake Ontario.

Now I know that another commonly used Mnemonic Memory Device for the Great Lakes is "HOMES," but "Super Man Helps Everyone" is even better because it's properly directional — you can start on the left and simply move to the right. The kids will get it right this way every single time.

BILL:
Seems like geography is perfect for this type of teaching method.

TOM:
Once I pre-tested a group of students by giving them a blank map of the United States. The average student correctly labeled six states: California, Florida, Texas, and usually three other states they visited. But after using my Mnemonic Memory Devices for 20 minutes a day, teaching just five states each day, the average student identified 48 of the 50 states. And my class was filled with ADHD children.

> *Medical and law students rely on these techniques. The rule of thumb is: "If you want someone to remember something long-term, then tell a joke about it, sing a song about it, or tell a story around it."*

Medical and law students rely on these techniques. The rule of thumb is: "If you want someone to remember something long-term, then tell a joke about it, sing a song about it, or tell a story around it." When it comes to the Mnemonic Memory Devices, it's the saying that stays in your long-term memory.

Mnemonic Devices are for all students. However, these devices can really save students with ADHD. They won't struggle to learn new material because the Mnemonic Devices are so user-friendly. In fact, I enlist my students — especially my ADHD children — in creating new Mnemonic Memory Devices.

These devices eliminate the distractibility factor in your ADHD kids. They're going to tune into the funny sayings, they're going to retain the material, and they will pay attention while you're teaching!

Points to remember from Chapter 17

▶ Mnemonic Memory Devices are great tools to use with all kids, but they're especially useful for ADHD kids.

▶ Encourage students to create their own funny sayings; they'll pay attention better and retain the material longer.

Teacher Quick Write #20

Write down one to three new Mnemonic Memory Devices you plan to use in your class. _____

_____

_____

#21 What are three Mnemonic Memory Devices you could ask your students to create? _____

_____

_____

_____

190

CHAPTER 18

12 ways to reach an ADHD child

Here are 12 ways to reach an ADHD child each and every day. This list was developed in part from an old worksheet entitled, "Ten ways to raise the self esteem of a child," (author unknown).

What this list presents is 12 easy, simple things you should do every day to connect with your ADHD students. Make a copy of them and tape them to the inside of your desk, lesson book, or some other convenient place where you'll see them frequently.

1. **Take their ideas and feelings seriously.**

   This is critical. Honestly assess your actions and improve your listening skills. The art of listening sounds easy, but takes a lot of diligence. Keep in mind the payoff for listening to an ADHD child is huge. Using Walk and Talk on a regular basis provides a great opportunity to listen seriously to kids.

2. **Define limits and rules clearly, and enforce them consistently.**

   Make sure you are crystal clear on your rules. If there is flexibility in your rules, make sure you are clear on how that flexibility will be applied to the rules. Think out loud and let your students eavesdrop in that conversation.

3. **Be a good role model.**
Let them see that you feel good about yourself. Also let them see that you make mistakes — and reveal how you learn from them.

4. **Teach them how to spend their time and money wisely.**

For example, you could turn a math lesson into a lesson on how to buy a car. Show them how to be smart consumers.

5. **Establish reasonable expectations.**

Give children reachable goals so that they can actually see, touch and feel success. You don't want to set the bar too high.

6. **Give them responsibility**.

By doing this, they will feel useful and valued. The responsibilities you assign can even be simple tasks. For example, the most hyperactive children in my classes are often in charge of staplers, glue sticks and all the school supplies. This provides a sense of purpose and responsibility that does them a world of good — and helps keep active children in line, too!

> *Give children reachable goals so that they can actually see, touch and feel success.*

7. **Be available.**

Give support when needed.

8. **Show them that what they do is important to you.**

Talk with them about their activities and interests.

9. **Express your values without pushing them onto your students.**

Emphasize your values on issues such as honesty, follow-through, commitment, and punctuality. Express those values in a casual manner as situations arise. **However, remember to keep matters of religion private.**

10. Spend time together.

Find activities that are mutually enjoyable between you and your ADHD students. Perhaps there is some structured free time in which you play chess with your ADHD student, or maybe a hangman-type word game, or go on a Walk and Talk.

11. Ask lots of questions to keep students involved.

Sample questions: "Well, what do *you* think about this?" "Compare this to something you've gone through personally."

12. Build a daily rapport with their parents.

Do this by calling parents twice as often with positive reports as phone calling regarding areas of concern.

Teacher Quick Write #22

How can I creatively teach my students to spend their time more wisely? _____

_____

_____

_____

_____

Points to remember from Chapter 18

▶ 12 Ways To Reach An ADHD Child Each And Every Day

1. Take their ideas seriously.

2. Define limits clearly.

3. Be a good role model.

4. Teach them to spend time and money wisely.

5. Establish reasonable expectations. Give children reachable goals so they can see, touch and feel success.

6. Give them responsibilities.

7. Be available.

8. Show them what they do is important to you.

9. Express your values (but keep religion private).

10. Spend time together.

11. Ask them lots of questions.

12. Build rapport with parents by making positive phone calls.

CHAPTER 19

Seven classroom set-up ideas to reduce ADHD-related problems

TOM:

You will eliminate many problems by setting up your classroom in creative, useful ways.

1. Use study carrels as a refuge and workspace for your ADHD children.

A study carrel is a desk that comes with its own walls. Most of the time your ADHD students will work at their own desks just like all the other kids, but it is useful to have a study carrel in another part of the classroom.

You can use this idea any number of ways. Perhaps the student self-monitors his behavior and goes to the carrel whenever he needs to move, or maybe the two of you decide on a prearranged hand signal that sends him to the carrel. In this way, the student is still part of the class but gets a little seclusion. You could have multiple study carrels in your room **and call it the "Quiet Study Area."** That way, there won't be a stigma attached to using the carrels.

BILL:

Will other kids feel slighted that they don't get to use the study carrels? Could it be seen as some sort of perk?

TOM:

Well, the other kids can use them, too, but what you'll have to do is find a way that makes it seem natural that your ADHD child is going there a lot. That will limit the number of trips the other kids make to the carrels. The other kids need to understand that you use your discretion as the teacher in deciding who uses the carrels and when.

2. Put up notes on the ceiling.

Another idea, which is fun and unconventional, is to put up notes on the ceiling with motivational messages, such as, *"Hey, let's get back to work!"* You could put up your weekly vocabulary words, multiplication tables, or grammar rules. Use tape or thumbtacks. Change the items posted on the ceiling each week.

Also, please realize that some schools may deem "notes on the ceiling" as a fire code violation. So, in that case, please comply with your school site rules.

3. Create a "Movement Path," or assign extra P.E.

A "Movement Path" may be used with younger children. It's an area in the back of the room where you have some space. It's for kids who are hyper and have lots of impulsive energy. Set up an area in the back of the room and make sure it doesn't distract the other students. If the Movement Path doesn't work out, consider assigning the student an extra P.E. class to work off excess energy. Here's one way — assign the student as a student assistant in the P.E. department.

4. Color-code as many things as possible.

When you color-code items, it organizes things for kids with ADHD. For example, my first period journals are all light blue, they're all numbered, and I keep them in the same place every day. For second period, they're all numbered, red-colored journals. Teach kids to color-code their own books and binders, too.

Being organized is often the difference between 'A' and 'B' students! And when the teacher is better organized, it means less stress on her, too.

5. Establish classroom procedures.

For example, do not write out a new bathroom pass whenever a student needs one. A better system is to have a permanent pass set up, and instruct the kids to give you a prearranged signal. Or have them sign a clipboard, take the pass, and then return and sign back in on the clipboard. Set up something that's consistent and regulated so that you're not interrupted needlessly. It will teach kids responsibility.

BILL:
How do you guard against overuse of a hall pass?

TOM:
I would work out a system, approved by your administrator, where each kid receives a total of five passes for the semester, and when they've used up their allotment, they've simply run out of passes. Just use the clipboard to tally bathroom use at the end of each day.

A student who must go to the restroom after using up his five passes, should be allowed to go, but he will owe five minutes during the lunch (or recess) time.

6. Reduce tattling with a "Positive Compliment Book."

TOM:
Set up a "Positive Compliment Book." Then you can tell your students, "Okay, I don't want to hear negative tattling — but I do want to hear positive tattling. So if you see anyone doing a great job or a kind deed, I want you to write it down in this book." (Of course, with high school students, I do not use words like "tattling" — instead, I use the phrase "put downs.")

What will happen is, some student will catch an ADHD child doing something good, and then you can read the entries in front of your class: "Hey, Spencer found that Ronnie was at the swings and waited for his turn, and even let Susie go ahead."

BILL:
Why is the compliment book important?

TOM: You are establishing a payoff for being good.

> **If a student is acting out as a way to get attention, he now understands the rules of the game have changed, and that he will now get more attention by being good.**

7. Increase homework compliance with "Homework Phone Calls."

TOM:
"Homework Phone Calls" work like this: Let's say your ADHD student can't remember his homework assignment. You have him call home from your classroom and leave himself a voice mail. It's simple and effective. The student simply dials his own phone number and says, "Hi, this is Steve, and my homework tonight is to do page 27, questions one through five, and also to write about these five animals."

If his mom gets home before he does, she can make note of the assignment. Or if he gets home first, all he has to do is to push the button on his home's voice mail to remember the assignment. As a twist to this, have the student call his parent at work to inform her of the assignment.

Another way is to set up a voice mail on a special homework phone line. On the special phone line you can have an outgoing message that contains an updated message about that day's particular assignment. It could say something like, "Hi, this is Miss Winters, your teacher. Your homework assignments for the week are _____."

Another method is to set up a "Homework Page" on your school's website. At schoolnotes.com, teachers set up their own web page and list useful information such as homework assignments and upcoming project deadlines.

These ideas alleviate the problem of parents saying that their child never has homework, or that the parents never received information the student was supposed to bring home. Just remember to be consistent and regularly update your voice mail or website.

Teacher Quick Write #23

- I can use study carrels in my class for . . .

_____

_____

_____

_____

#24 Five things in my class I can color code are . . .

_____

_____

_____

_____

_____

Points to remember from Chapter 19

► Consider these seven ideas on setting up your classroom to reduce ADHD-related behavior:

- Use study carrels in the back of the room.

- Put notes on the ceiling.

- Create a "Movement Path" or assign extra P.E. (or assign the student a P.E. aide).

- Color-code everything.

- Establish an effective bathroom pass procedure.

- Create a compliment book.

- Have forgetful students call home with their homework assignments.